Pebbles from Fallen Leaf Lake
and Other Motivational Moments

MAVEN
MARK
BOOKS

Pebbles from Fallen Leaf Lake
and Other Motivational Moments

Sheryl Hughey

Linda –
  "Dreaming" is your specialty – keep
believing in others and your dreams ahead
will continue to come true.
    Thanks for your leadership –
      Love, Sheryl

Published by:
MavenMark Books, LLC
www.MavenMarkBooks.com
Please contact the publisher for information on quantity discounts for
educational purposes.

ISBN: 978-1-59598-081-6

Printed in the United States of America.

Table of Contents

Foreword

More often than not, seemingly irrelevant events and moments in our lives pass by without us giving them a second thought. What is the significance of trudging to a woodshed, through the snow, multiple times a day, to haul back armloads of firewood—only to watch it burn down hours later? Or, even sillier, what is the deeper meaning of the "perfect" glass of lemonade while on a family camping trip? Surely, there's nothing more to driving past telephone poles suspended by wires along a lonely stretch of highway, other than what it is?

What an enlightening and humbling surprise when I began my own journey to Sheryl Hughey's beloved Fallen Leaf Lake. There, Sheryl's recollections of her family's adventures and her own everyday observations jumped into my heart as seemingly fleeting moments or memories rippled across the lake waters and sent meaning and wisdom down my spine. Each story, profoundly detailed to the sensory elements of smell, touch, and sight, is so vivid, you can't help but BE there.

As I breathlessly climbed Mount Cathedral with Sheryl, her father and mother, or dined on decadent biscuits and gravy for breakfast, or joined Sheryl as she climbed a tree 100 feet above the forest ground, this beautiful book unwittingly became a personal rediscovery of the simple, oh-so-long forgotten, and easily discarded important things of life.

Each poignant vignette concludes with a "Pebble to Ponder." Skillfully presented in the form of innocent questions like, "What if you took one more step when you thought you couldn't?" or "What's in your personal storage unit of energy, are your shelves stocked with all that you will need when rations of self fulfillment are low?" I found myself answering – "That's the point!"

Brilliantly incorporating exercises to flex those muscles for discovering purpose, creativity, productivity, service attitude, and efficiency, Sheryl's simple book rapidly evolves into a hands-on, no-frills workbook for personal development, life skills assessment, and professional enrichment.

Readers fortunate enough to experience Fallen Leaf Lake and ponder over a pebble or two will grow and rediscover themselves, their joy, their "why," through the stories and practical, thought-provoking exercises. What a tool this would serve for corporations who want an "easy read" to get their teams to find the "why" that will surely enhance and manifest positive, productive, and contributing individuals.

Take a deep breath, smell the pines, and listen to the ripples of wisdom at Fallen Leaf Lake.

Connie Tang
President, JAFRA USA
JAFRA Cosmetics International, Inc.

Acknowledgments

Heartfelt and sincere thanks are due to so many:

To my loving parents, John and Shirley Hughey, who recognized the value of annual family vacations and discovered our paradise of Fallen Leaf Lake—To my sister, Diana, for helping me remember the details and find the photos—To my brother, John, and new "sister," Suzanne, for opening your hearts and healing our family just when we needed you—To Brenda Huckle and Genuine Image Photography—To Kira Henschel and MavenMark Books. WOW!—To my dear friend Rosalind Boukis who grew up hearing about Fallen Leaf Lake as we rode our bikes together to school in sixth grade and for the talents and promotional materials from her company, Advertising Magic—To Connie Tang and JAFRA Cosmetics for allowing me to grow into my dreams and become a better version of myself—To Bill and Barbara Craven for your legacy—To Jax, Judi, and Patsy for all our Meeting Room No. 5 sessions—To Sheila, for cheering all the way from England—To Alex, for all the joy and love you add to my life and for teaching me what commitment means. And, to my right arm, Jane, for listening to ideas and helping bring them to life, and for lovingly believing.

Our family Paradise—Fallen Leaf Lake

PART ONE:
The Day Time Stood Still

*Your work is to discover your world
and then with all your heart give yourself to it.*
—Buddha

The Call

I'll never forget the brisk and sunny February morning in 2004 and the cell phone conversation with my mom. In a rush to do a little shopping and take in an early movie between business trips, I hastily hit the speed dial button on my cell phone. I remember feeling content, grateful and connected to my new home in Maple Valley, Washington. I remember feeling optimistic and at peace with myself and the universe. But that feeling was not meant to last.

"Hi, Mom—I got your message. I just got home last night from Orlando—what's up?"

"I have some bad news. I have liver cancer. It's terminal. I love you. And, I'm sorry."

The words rang through my head, pierced my heart, and in that instant, time stood still. In that instant, I connected with a lifetime of memories, lessons my mother had taught me, coupled with the shock and horror of her news. In that instant, I was a young teen again—sitting on the wooden porch at Sherman Cabin five days into our family vacation in the Sierra Nevada mountains, on a warm July day, watching Mom do her needlework and begging her to let my sister and me go swimming. In that instant, I was back at Fallen Leaf Lake, our family vacation spot—the place Mom described as "Paradise."

The Discovery

Mom and Dad discovered Fallen Leaf Lake by accident in the summer of 1965 when I was only a couple of months old. They had driven to Lake Tahoe from our home in Concord, California, only to find the campground at Emerald Bay full. My resourceful father asked for an alternate place to pitch our tent—and a tiny, little known campground at Fallen Leaf Lake was recommended.

Nestled between Emerald Bay and South Lake Tahoe, Fallen Leaf Lake in those days would have been nearly as difficult to find as it is today. A small road sign along Highway 89 is all that marks the turn-off—blink and the next stop is Emerald Bay. Just a few miles from the shores of South Lake Tahoe, Fallen Leaf Lake, or "The Leaf" as many lifetime alumni call it, is a small oblong lake, five miles long by a mile wide at its broadest point. "The Leaf" is protected and secluded beneath the towering mountain peaks of Mount Cathedral and Mount Tallac. In the gilded age of the 1920s and 1930s, Fallen Leaf Lake acted as gatekeeper to Glen Alpine Spring—an old western resort destination. Today, the same road leads to a main trailhead for a serious backpacker's Shangri-La known as Desolation Wilderness.

As Dad turned off the highway onto Fallen Leaf Road over forty years ago, I doubt he knew the treasure that awaited him. I doubt he considered the significance of what this discovery would mean for our family. The five-mile drive to Fallen Leaf Lodge has always challenged even the bravest drivers—a one-lane road with twists, blind turns and pot holes. As Dad crept along, the road became narrower, thick pine forests and lush meadows lining both sides. When the crystal-clear, blue water of Fallen Leaf Lake finally peeked out from behind the trees, surrounded by mountains on every side and revealed its pristine beauty and sheltered coves, I can imagine both Mom and Dad gasping in awe. I can imagine their eyes straining to take it all in. I can imagine them smiling at each other.

Over the years—in fact, every summer of my life until I went to college—my family made the journey back to Fallen Leaf Lake for our family vacation. Our vacations at the lake evolved as we grew. In the early 1970s, Mom, Dad, my sister Diana and I spent our summer vacations camping in a tent along the Alpine Creek. A camper/RV was our first upgrade, although we remained loyal to the creek-side campsites. Our desire for more comfortable camping, private bathrooms, showers, and electricity eventually led us to move up to renting cabins. From the rustic cabin Cathedral View, to the more modern Meadowlark, and finally to the privately owned Sherman Cabin, our family vacations at Fallen Leaf Lake became a constant—something we knew would always be. For two weeks each summer, Fallen Leaf Lake was home—a home that didn't change with time, progress, and technology.

Our annual retreats to Fallen Leaf Lake became a touchstone for my family—and for me. Each year, I'd return to specific trees, or rocks, or spots on the beach to find nothing had changed. I am my mother's daughter, so naturally Fallen Leaf Lake became my paradise, too—a place that lived vibrantly in my mind during the long year between summer visits. Even now, I can close my eyes and smell the fragrant pines, hear the songbirds and grasshoppers chirping in stereo, and feel the soft Sierra breeze on my face. I am more connected and drawn to Fallen Leaf Lake than I am to my hometown Concord, California. At Fallen Leaf Lake, I feel strong, independent and connected. At Fallen Leaf Lake, I become curious, observant, reverent, and grateful. At Fallen Leaf Lake, my heart swells with love, and I feel peace and serenity. For me, Fallen Leaf Lake is heaven on earth.

One of my favorite rituals as a young girl was to collect pebbles from the beach down by the Lodge's public dock as Mom and Dad supervised. The sand along the shore of the lake was coarse and contained small bits of rock and "fool's gold." Wading into the crystalline water up to my knees, I'd bend down and scoop up a handful of sand and stones, then hold it above the water studying the color and texture of the tiny bits of stone. I'd carry my loot to the beach and dump the soggy pile on the drier sand. Carefully, I'd dig through the mixture, selecting the most perfect pebbles to be my treasure. My eyes danced as I eagerly explored my pile of sand. The fool's gold sparkled in the summer sun, and I wondered how the adults could be so calm talking and lying about on the swimming dock when all around them was a gold mine!

Once I had extracted the pebbles from the mound of sand, I'd return to the water and sink my pebble-laden hands beneath the surface. I'd part my fingers slightly and rinse my pebbles, letting any remaining sandy bits fall back into the water. Once back on the beach with my clean pebbles, I'd examine each more closely, saving those that were different that the others I'd already found. At the end of the day, I'd camouflage my treasure of pebbles—unique in color, shape and size—under bark or leaves so I could return the next day to add to my Fallen Leaf Lake treasure.

The Promise

Less than three weeks after the cell phone conversation with Mom, on the day time stood still, I sat in her hospital room holding her hand. We gently laughed, recalling sweet memories and countless moments of time spent together, freed from the pressure of everyday life, at Fallen Leaf Lake.

Both strong-willed and independent, Mom and I frequently butted heads. She set high expectations for me and wanted to spare me from the typical heartache and pain of growing up. I resisted her protecting arm and yearned for the freedom and independence to make my own way. She wanted to hold on—to slow time down—to keep me near her for just a little longer. And I—looking forward to the future, dreaming of my life ahead, always anticipating what was next—wanted time to move faster.

Fallen Leaf Lake became our place of connection, where the drama of mother and daughter relationships took a holiday for a couple of weeks every summer, where we could just be content…be at peace…be ourselves. Time slowed to a pace that was marked by starlit conversations, walks along the creek to the falls, and family games of *Aggravation* and *Pinochle*. Mom and I laughed more at Fallen Leaf Lake. We treasured each other more at Fallen Leaf Lake. We enjoyed slow passing time together at Fallen Leaf Lake.

But the sweetness of our paradise couldn't mask today's reality. Mom was slipping away, day by day—the cancer aggressively attacking her weakening body. Mom was never good at letting go or saying good-bye, other traits she passed along to me. As she lay in her hospital bed, her face suddenly tightened and her brow furrowed as if she had a very serious matter on her mind. With tears gathering at the corners of her eyes, she gently looked in mine: "I never got around to writing my book," she said wistfully. "Promise me you'll write one instead."

Swallowing hard and fighting back hot tears of my own, I squeezed her hand and whispered "I promise." With that, Mom's expression softened and she drifted into sleep.

The Inspiration

That evening, as my sister and I left Mount Diablo Hospital in an attempt to find some respite from our sadness, I thought again about Fallen Leaf Lake—and my pebbles. Throughout all the years and visits to Fallen Leaf Lake, I had collected another kind of pebble—pebbles in the form of lessons and experiences. These colorful and unique pebbles are treasured bits and moments of inspiration and clarity that came from simple days at my "Leaf." Many of these pebbles have served to guide me in my life and my career.

Mom wasn't successful in her quest to spare me some of the harder lessons life teaches. Like many, I've been bruised by the mistakes of young adulthood and the real consequences of poor choices. As a young college graduate, I found myself working as a receptionist for a construction company in Salt Lake City—not exactly the dream I had imagined for myself. A decade later, I found myself divorced, single with a cat for companionship, managing a team of instructors and sales executives in the IT computer training industry. Today, I work as a National Training Manager for JAFRA Cosmetics International. After too many years of renting apartments and town homes, I finally purchased my first home nearly six years ago. As my career and life have evolved, the pebbles have provided me with insights and clarity to allow me to better handle a family challenge, a career crisis, or struggles with the teams I manage.

We've complicated our lives, culture and society to the brink of chaos. Multi-tasking, career ladders, commuter traffic, cell phones, email, television, politics—volumes have been written on the impacts our complicated lives wreak on our health, happiness and success. For me, pausing and reflecting on the lessons from the pebbles serve as a reminder of simplicity—offering clarity, alternatives or perspective. Just as the pebbles have unique patterns, edges and multiple surfaces, so do our challenges, struggles and opportunities in life. By turning the pebble over, we often find new ideas, new characteristics, new options, and new solutions.

Memories of my magical Fallen Leaf Lake blanket my mind and heart like the thousands of tiny pebbles lining the beach of our lake. And so, I dedicate this collection of pebbles to my mother, Shirley Claire Chase Hughey, who lovingly gave me countless gifts throughout our life together. Mom instilled deep within me the belief that each of us possesses special gifts and can accomplish anything we set our minds to. She was my first and most beloved teacher, showing me the value of creating precious memories from each hour, each day, and every summer vacation at our family paradise of Fallen Leaf Lake.

Sheryl Hughey
Maple Valley, Washington
May 2009

Our protected cove at Sherman Cabin

PART TWO:
The Pebbles

Within our reach
Lies every path
We ever dream of taking.

Within our power
Lies every step
We ever dream of making.

Within our range
Lies every joy
We ever dream of seeing.

Within ourselves
Lies everything
We ever dream of being.
      —Unknown

Fallen Leaf Lodge brochure, ca 1970

PARADISE
Mr. and Mrs. Bill Craven

I wish people would come to the mountains
and appreciate them for what they are.
—Bill Craven

It was the guests who made running the Lodge so special.
—Barbara Craven

Fallen Leaf Lodge, a private vacation facility owned by the Craven family, sat humbly at the south end of Fallen Leaf Lake. The Lodge property was dusted with rustic cabins and campsites. The best campsites were hidden above the lake, creek-side near Alpine Falls, and offered affordable family vacationing at $5.00 per day. The Cravens also managed a small hotel, which boasted ten rooms, each with a magnificent view of the lake, for only $25 per night. A general store, marina, recreation hall, and coffee shop rounded out Fallen Leaf Lodge's amenities.

Fallen Leaf Lodge bore silent tribute to efficiency, simplicity, and family. From my elementary-school-aged eyes, the Lodge seemed to run without effort—the store was always stocked with my favorite treats—and blocks of ice arrived on large trucks the very day we needed more. The ladies who ran the post office knew everyone by name. Mr. Craven was often seen in his green pick-up truck, the name "Walter" painted in white letters on the hood, with shovels, rakes, saws and beat-up aluminum trash cans carefully perched in the back. College students worked the store, the coffee shop, and organized activities for the children visiting the lake. Much like pushing the pause button while listening to music, the Lodge seemed to pick up each year exactly as it had left off—a tribute to a simpler time.

In assembling memories and recollections from Fallen Leaf Lake, I was able to connect with Bill and Barbara Craven during a short visit in September, 2008. To my delight and surprise, they clearly remembered my mother and father, and our family's long history of summer vacations at the Lodge. I was eager to learn more about their amazing life at Fallen Leaf Lake, and the Cravens and I enjoyed a wonderful conversation from which my appreciation of their service to so many families and the extent of their labor of love was confirmed.

Mr. and Mrs. Bill Craven inherited the care of Fallen Leaf Lodge in 1972 when Bill's mother became too ill to continue running her beloved resort. Bill's mother and aunt managed both the original Fallen Leaf Lodge (which is now Camp Stanford) and the Housekeeping Camp, which became Fallen Leaf Lodge when the original resort was sold to Stanford University in the late 1950s. Bill Craven's grandfather was one of the first developers to arrive in the beautiful Fallen Leaf Lake area, settling there in the 1890s. He established a boy's camp and later, started Fallen Leaf Lodge between 1905 and 1907 after enough of his friends observed, "This would be a great place for a vacation resort!"

Before coming to live at Fallen Leaf Lake full time, Bill Craven worked as a mining engineer and consultant, while his wife Barbara labored as a school teacher in Sutter Creek, California. Mr. and Mrs. Craven lovingly managed Fallen Leaf Lodge for fourteen years from 1972 to 1986 when, very painfully for the Cravens, the Lodge closed down due to the costs involved with a major sewer project required by the county. Both Mr. and Mrs. Craven still live year round in their beautiful home on the shore of Fallen Leaf Lake in the shadow of Mount Cathedral. Although they've traveled to many other lovely locations, neither can imagine living anywhere else.

Mr. and Mrs. Craven both played vital roles in ensuring that all of their guests enjoyed their time in the mountains. Mr. Craven rose early every morning, and before breakfast, performed many essential tasks. With garbage bag in hand, Bill Craven walked the length of the Lodge's lake front to collect any trash carelessly left from the day before, or to repair the damage if animals had rummaged through or knocked over trash cans in the night. He wanted to make sure that when his guests arose, they saw the lake the way it was intended, pristine and rubbish-free. Checking over the night watchman's log and making sure the hot water heaters were pre-heating completed Bill's early-morning rounds. Heading to the coffee shop and the employee dining room, Mr. Craven joined the thirty or more seasonal employees who ran Fallen Leaf Lodge for breakfast before returning to his daily duties.

Mrs. Barbara Craven's responsibilities included supervising the housekeeping staff during the summer months and managing all the reservations for the following year in the off-season. Each year, Mrs. Craven trained the college girls who worked as the housekeeping staff to properly clean the toilets, change the linens, and clean the windows of every property at the Lodge.

"The view of the lake was the most important thing for me," says Mrs. Craven. So, each week when families would vacate and before a new family arrived, the housekeeping staff cleaned the windows and removed the moths and bugs from the lamps and window sills. Every guest was treated to a clean accommodation that passed Mrs. Craven's careful inspection.

Not surprisingly, once families experienced the Cravens' hospitality, they were eager to return. Preference was given to returning families, and most submitted choices for vacation weeks for the following summer before leaving for home each year. In the days before computers, Mrs. Craven collected the cards and reservation requests and spread them out on the living room floor to assemble the summer schedule.

"We began taking reservations over the phone in February, and required an advance deposit to hold a reservation," Mrs. Craven recalls. When conflicts arose, Mrs. Craven worked tirelessly to find alternatives and solutions. Sometimes a returning family would invite a new family to join them during their requested week, and Mrs. Craven would search to find a way to accommodate the newcomers in paradise. Keeping track of the master schedule haunted Mrs. Craven all day and even as she slept, and she would sometimes wake in the middle of the night worrying that she had double-booked a cabin or campsite with two families for the same week.

Commenting on what they loved most about running Fallen Leaf Lodge, both Mr. and Mrs. Craven agreed it was their guests. "We looked forward to the people—watching the families and children grow up and return year after year," reflected Mrs. Craven. Bill Craven found the diversity of visitors to the lodge amazing and rewarding. Aerospace engineers from Lockheed camped alongside doctors and families who worked in farmer's markets in San Francisco. "The common denominator in the whole thing was that all these people came to the mountains to experience what the mountains had to offer."

For Mr. and Mrs. Craven, the mountains that shelter Fallen Leaf Lake offer majesty, nature, simplicity, beauty, relaxation away from hectic lifestyles, and connection—where strangers became friends sitting around a campfire singing songs and telling stories.

Living at Fallen Leaf Lake year round is a life Mr. and Mrs. Craven wouldn't trade. Mrs. Craven enjoys the quiet, watching nature and the lake change from season to season, the way the lake looks right before a winter storm. They enjoy being removed from the noise, content to venture into town only once per week. "It's not a normal life," she comments, but they clearly love it. Bill Craven notes that while Fallen Leaf is not a very hospitable location for the four or five months of harsh winter weather each year, he has become a keen observer of the subtle changes offered by the nature around him. His favorite season is spring, when misty green fern and grass and delicate spring blossoms fill the valley with renewal and hope.

Pebble to Ponder

It's difficult to describe the intensity of my feelings that accompany each visit to Fallen Leaf Lake. Happiness, peace and awe, coupled with the breathtaking splendor of the mountains, trees and water, create a place unlike any other I've visited. What I did not appreciate until my recent visit with the Cravens was the extent to which my Fallen Leaf paradise was nurtured and watched over by loving hands and hearts. Creating a paradise for others is the legacy left to so many by Bill and Barbara Craven.

They worked without glitz, glamour, or fame and were profoundly concerned that each guest would have a splendid and pristine experience at the Lodge. Backstage, away from the spotlight of the lake, the Cravens were quietly brilliant. Pouring their hearts and energy into the Lodge, the Cravens gave their best day after day, week after week, year after year. Their efforts and dedication created an atmosphere, a culture of family and friendship.

Working at Fallen Leaf Lodge meant doing more than the minimum. While it may have been adequate to clean the windows once each month or simply empty the trash cans that lined the public beach area, Bill and Barbara Craven chose to go the extra mile, to pay attention to the small details, to delight children visitors with scavenger hunts and adult visitors with slide shows of wildflowers and tips for exploring the numerous mountain trails. The Cravens watched over countless components, and offered their generous, heartfelt care to all who came to enjoy the mountains.

Creating paradise—a place of beauty, happiness, delight, or contentment—is a choice any of us can make. Paradise can exist anywhere where, like Bill and Barbara Craven, we:

- Work without concern of glitz, glamour or reward
- Pour our hearts and energy into something we love
- Give our best effort every day
- Create a supportive atmosphere
- Pay close attention to details
- Give generously from our hearts

As a young girl, I knew little of the work and dedication required to create such a special and magical retreat. All I saw was the beauty. I did not see bed linens hanging out to dry on Mrs. Craven's watch. I did not see Mr. Craven dutifully checking the water level at the reservoir above the falls. My family and the countless others who visited during the summer season at Fallen Leaf Lodge were the recipients of the service offered without thought of fame or reward, by the generous hearts of Bill and Barbara Craven, stewards of paradise.

PURPOSE
Mount Cathedral

We all need something to believe in, something for which we can have whole-hearted enthusiasm. We need to feel that our life has meaning; that we are needed in this world.
—Hannah Senesh

Each day when my family and I awoke at Fallen Leaf Lake, the magnificent splendor of Mount Cathedral greeted us. With rugged edges and huge boulders, it seemed to change shape as we peered at it from different angles. Near its crest, a year-round snow pack seemed untouchable—and as a girl, I often wondered if I could see the snow close up, would I see Santa's foot prints? In the hottest part of the afternoon, the mountain provided us with cool and lasting shade as it swallowed the sun behind its peak.

Mount Cathedral—our ever-present backdrop at Fallen Leaf Lake.

Among my earliest memories of Fallen Leaf Lake was gazing up at Mount Cathedral, studying its seeming endless changes in color and shape and dreaming about climbing to the top. This mountain touched the sky and stretched all the way down to the shores of Fallen Leaf Lake. A solid sentinel, it guards all who come near. At the end of each day, Mount Cathedral collects the sun and gently puts her to sleep behind its rocky and unmoving peak.

One morning in the early 1970s, I woke at dawn to watch Dad as he gathered up his canteen, small backpack, hiking stick, and cream-colored floppy hat. He was off to climb Mount Cathedral again, this time up its jagged face. As he laced up his hiking boots, I walked over and placed my hand on his knee.

"Daddy, when will I be old enough to climb the mountain?"

His simple answer found a place in my heart and settled there. "Sweetheart, it's not easy to climb a mountain. You need to be strong. You need to decide you want to make it to the top, then build up your strength. One day, when you're ready—together, we'll climb that mountain."

I stayed near our campsite that day, studying the mountainside, searching the massive rocks with the family binoculars, wanting more than anything to see my dad climbing. I imagined I would spot him and call out to him, and that the soft breeze would carry my greeting up to him. Hearing my voice, he would pause look down at me and smile and wave. I searched the mountain all day, looking for Dad, and thinking about my journey to the top of the mountain…someday.

I wasted no time when we returned home after our vacation that year. Armed with my father's encouragement, I was determined to build up my strength and endurance. I rode my bike and took training walks around the neighborhood. I carried my canteen to and from school to practice drinking enough water. Then, when we returned to Fallen Leaf Lake the following summer, Dad and I took shorter hikes to help me build my endurance at the higher mountain altitudes. Mom picked up on my enthusiasm and decided she too would like to see the top of MountCathedral, so she joined us on these training hikes.

My preparation and training lasted for three long years. Finally, on my tenth birthday I received my first pair of hiking boots—a signal from Dad that he believed I was strong enough to hike to the summit of Mount Cathedral.

And so it happened that on July 11, 1975, I climbed my first mountain! Dad, Mom and I rose before dawn and with butterflies in my stomach, began the ten-mile, round-trip journey that would take us nearly twelve hours to complete. As we started off down the trail, level and smooth, I remember thinking: "This is going to be easy!" But it wasn't too far along that we encountered our first obstacle: huge boulders from an old rock slide blocking the trail. Many of these rocks were taller than my four-foot-tall body, so Dad wedged himself between two of the boulders and lifted and swung me up to the top of the rock. It only took us a couple of tries to get the hang of this gymnastic maneuver, and in no time, we were jumping over the boulders like limber mountain goats.

The trail gradually became steeper and sunnier. As the morning wore on, we took more frequent breaks along the trail, munching on beef jerky and trail mix, and sipping from our supply of water. All the while, the view of our beloved Fallen Leaf Lake kept us company as we climbed. Dad hummed and whistled as we walked, and my short legs struggled to keep up with his pace. Eventually, the trail changed from the steep switchbacks to a wooded alpine forest path that wound and rose until we came to a huge clearing, from which we could gaze upon the vast snow pack and the summit!

Snowfall had been heavier the previous winter and the snow pack covering the trail to the summit was much larger than I imagined. I gazed at the shiny snow, squinting and searching it for footprints. Dad quickly outlined an alternate route around the snowy obstacle and we set off again, determined to reach the summit by noon. Mom and I followed with a mix of wonder and fatigue, one step at a time, until finally… finally we arrived at the simple, wood-carved sign that read: Mount Cathedral Summit: 6,626 ft.

Disappointed and confused would be two words that described my feelings at that moment. As I looked around, an expanse of boulders spread out in every direction around me. What I did not see was the view I had been dreaming of—the one looking down on Fallen Leaf Lake.

Dad saw my face and gently laughed: "Not much further…c'mon, Sheri. I've got salami sandwiches and nectarines!"

Putting on my best mountain goat legs and finding a burst of anticipation, I set off after Dad across the field of boulders, leaping from rock to rock, careful to land in the center of the rocks as some of them wiggled under my feet. The wind became gustier with each step; the sun was nearly directly overhead and reflected summer heat off the grey black boulders. I kept one eye on my feet and one eye on Dad as I galloped along. I hummed a tune in my head: "Almost there. I'm going to make it!"

I'd spent my young lifetime of summers looking up to the summit of Mount Cathedral in wonder, imagining what I'd be able to see from the top. And here I was, looking down at Fallen Leaf Lake. Mom, Dad, and I sat near a homemade flag pole a previous hiker had wedged between the boulders to mark the best view and gazed out at the wonder of our paradise. In the distance, I could see nearly all of Lake Tahoe, its blue water touching the far horizon. Behind me, the gently rolling valleys and lakes of Desolation Wilderness seemed wild and inviting. Beneath me, speckling the blue water of Fallen Leaf Lake, I could see tiny sails and the white lines of water churned by motor boats. I put my hand to my ear, straining to hear the hum of the engines, but they were like silent toys on the water below.

I grinned from ear to ear, the wind lashing my hair. I heard Dad laughing and looked over to see him and Mom smiling at me—we had made it!

After years of dreaming, striving and building, together, over 30 years ago, Dad, Mom, and I had spent the day climbing a mountain. Dad was there to support and encourage us when Mom and I became tired (and cranky). On that warm July day, from the hard-won summit, we enjoyed a breathtaking view, the sweetest nectarines I'd ever tasted, and a lingering feeling of satisfying accomplishment.

Pebble to Ponder

Setting goals—reaching company targets and quotas, saving for our kids' college education, buying a home—are all examples of mountains in our lives. It's not enough to simply set a goal or be told what the expected sales achievement is for the fiscal year. It's in the connection to the *why* behind our goal that drives and directs our efforts. The *why* is our purpose, the reason behind our dreams, our connection to our spiritual selves.

When we are able to visualize the top of the mountain, our destination, our purpose, we are equipping ourselves with the resources needed to climb it. Visualizing our destinations and the achievement of goals is the key to success. Rather than focusing on what *is*, we can instead focus on that we desire or *how we want things to be*. We must paint a picture in our mind of our destination: what it will look like, feel like, taste like, smell like.

Connecting to our purpose is a steady motivator as we journey through life. It keeps us going when the trail becomes steep, when the sun burns hot, when our water supply runs low. In any endeavor, the *how-to's*—our methods, our activities—contribute only a fraction toward our ultimate achievement. Remember the 80:20 rule? In this case, only 20 percent is in the how-to's; 80 percent is in the *why*.

We strengthen our connection to our *why*'s not only by visualizing our life from the top of the mountain, but also by connecting our purpose to the *larger-than-me* desires, the ways in which we wish to leave the world and our human family better than we found it.

Additionally, like my dad taught me, we need to build up our strength or set mini-goals or milestones that cause us to reach beyond what is comfortable and easy. The comfort zone is a drug most of us are addicted to. Often we move through life, locked in our powerful daily routines. Sometimes with regret, we wake up one day to find years have passed while we've been on autopilot.

The drive to create more for ourselves is a strong motivator. The challenge lies channeling our desires to actually creating it. A common refrain is that we are either in a state of growth or decay—there is no such thing as stability. Sometimes the summit seems so far away that it's easy to become discouraged by slow and almost indistinguishable progress. Therefore, to reach the summit, we must begin by building our strength—gaining momentum in the accomplishment of daily steps toward the achievement of our goals.

What ONE thing can you do today that will move you closer to achieving your destination? To push forward, to do a little more today than yesterday, to stretch—all essential steps required to reach the summits of our dreams.

Finally, as we build strength, remember, we don't climb alone. Regardless of our circumstances, I believe each of us has a cheering section. We have people to whom we are connected who lift us up and walk beside us on our journeys. Who cheers for you? Who questions you when you let yourself off the hook or back off from a goal? Whom can you reach out to and invite to climb with you?

In reaching our destinations in life, the reward is so much sweeter when we share it …and together we'll climb that mountain!

Give yourself the gift of reflecting on your PURPOSE. Explore what you really, really, really want. Determine without a single doubt, your *why*. Visualize what life will look like, taste like, be like once you are fully living your purpose.

July 11, 1975—Sheri and Dad share a satisfying moment at Mount Cathedral summit

Dad chopping wood at Fallen Leaf Lake,

PRESERVATION
Woodshed

Improve your spare moments and
they will become the brightest gems in your life.
—Ralph Waldo Emerson

Each December, I relish my holiday break. My annual work projects wind down along with my regional budget, and my thoughts turn to festivities, friends and feasting. The holidays for me are a chance to spend slowly passing hours in the company of family and friends. Together, laughing gently, catching up, sipping a festive holiday beverage mark the short winter days and long chilly nights. Snuggly evenings by firelight, card games and jigsaw puzzles while the Seattle rain drips steadily outside balance out the more festive holiday gatherings.

A few years ago, on the day after Christmas, my family journeyed to Mount Rainer and a rustic A-frame cabin in the woods. The drive from Maple Valley takes less than two hours, but leaving the metropolitan suburbs behind for the fern- and pine-covered landscape near Mount Rainier, we discovered a relaxing backdrop for our holiday get-away. The cabin is high on charm and warm blankets, but boasts no phone, no cable TV reception, no high-speed or dial-up Internet access. Even my cell phone found no signal. Ahhhh…. Heaven!

A typical Pacific Northwest rain storm forecasted steady cold rain in the city. With the elevation change from sea level, up at Mount Rainier, on the day we arrived, it began to snow and by the next morning, we had a fresh foot of white, fluffy stuff. Snowbound without a snow plow, and without any set appointments or reservations, we settled in for several glorious days of solitude with good friends and family. We ate a lot of comfort food. The entire cabin filled with the aroma of my famous lasagna, flavored heavily with fresh garlic and rosemary, dripping with melted mozzarella cheese and homemade meat sauce. Breakfast included freshly baked muffins, steaming hot from the oven, scrambled eggs with sausage and bacon—the works! We played board games galore. We read. We talked. We soaked in the steaming hot Jacuzzi while it snowed all around us. We held a world-class snowball fight and sledded down untouched white hills. We stayed toasty warm inside the cabin with the help of an old-fashioned wood stove. And the best amenity of all at our Shangri-la in the woods, out in back of the cabin, about 20 feet or so from the door, sat a woodshed filled to overflowing with dry wood to feed the stove.

Trekking to the woodshed several times a day became a highlight of the trip for me. The creaky woodshed door opened easily to reveal the smell of cedar and pine—the fuel we needed to keep the cabin comfortable. With joyful effort, I'd tromp back and forth from the cabin to the woodshed with armloads of firewood. My family enjoyed making a game out of it—"How many trips to the woodshed does it take to have enough wood for the day?" I'd stack the wood inside the front door of our A-frame in neat little rows near the raised stone hearth that held the wood stove. When the stash of wood started getting low, someone would pipe up "Sheri, time to go to the woodshed!"

I found myself keeping a constant eye on the stack of wood inside the cabin. I developed a regular need to connect with the woodshed, to shield my hands with sturdy gloves and march out to the woodshed to collect more of its treasure. This ritual became a source of amusement for my friends and family, who questioned the necessity of more wood—"Don't you think we have enough?" My desire to PRESERVE the supply of wood ensured in my mind that the toasty atmosphere inside the cabin would not be at risk during our stay.

Pebble to Ponder

What is the woodshed in your life? Where are the places you store your emotional energy reserve? How often do you replenish it? Are you dependent on it? Do you joyfully engage in the effort needed to fill and maintain your neatly stacked piles of dry wood? Are you reluctant to take from its abundance when opportunities grow cold?

My daily treks to the woodshed kept the stove from running low or completely out of fuel. The key to preserving the fuel were the consistent and regular treks to replenish our supply. Whether in the wilds of Washington or in our urban homes, each day, we wake to a fresh supply of twenty-four hours to fill in any way we choose. Carving out a fraction of that gift of time (even $1/24^{th}$ of it—one hour) to replenish our reserves of mental and physical energy can go a long way toward our effectiveness and feelings of productivity and competence.

Unfortunately, replenishing our woodpile often falls down on the priority list after all the other *have-to's* and *should-do's* that clutter our days. Our best intentions to exercise our bodies and fill our minds with positive energy give way to the pressing demands of work, family, and the other urgent obligations on our calendars.

The best way I've found to make replenishing energy and PRESERVING our supply of wood for the stove is to schedule the time to do so with as much urgency as eating, sleeping or filling the car with gasoline.

When we make the effort to carve out time to preserve our fuel supply, we develop a powerful habit. A wonderful book, *The Power of Focus* by Jack Canfield, Mark Victor Hansen and Les Hewitt, provides a thorough discussion of the power habits have on our lives. Habits are things we do so often they become easy. In terms of behavior, when we persist at performing a new behavior over and over again, eventually the behavior becomes automatic—a habit.

We each have times of day when we are more alert and able to perform at our peaks. For me, it's first thing in the morning. My most productive work days are those when, before I turn on the computer or return one phone call, I spend 30-40 minutes reading and learning from expert leaders. This activity replenishes my desire to continue to learn and grow. These precious minutes spent in quiet reflection prepare my mind and fortify my resolve to use creative new solutions to the challenges that pop up in my work day. And if I really want to have a stellar and productive day, I add a 30- to 40-minute physical workout to that early-morning routine.

When I justify that "I don't have time to exercise today," my mind works slower and my body aches after hours of sitting at the computer, on an airplane, or in the office. Conversely, when I make that little extra effort to spend less than 1/24th of my day in physical exercise, the benefits far outweigh the cost of time.

Spending time on the activities that replenish our reserves of energy and enthusiasm keep us prepared for the sudden storms in life. Because we had been provided with a ample reserve of energy at our A-frame cabin in the woods, the blizzard was easily endured. In fact, our cozy and content feelings, our toes warm from the red hot coals was made possible knowing we could rely on the fuel in our woodshed. Worry seemed as far away as the bustling noise of the city.

Alpine Creek

PATTERNS
Creek

A journey of a thousand miles begins with a single step.
—Chinese Proverb

In the dry and sunny Sierra Nevada mountain range, cool, clear and nourishing water takes center stage. Dependent on the snow pack from previous winters, water levels at Fallen Leaf Lake teetered between abundant and scarce. Years of drought would suddenly end with a heavy winter and the following summer, we'd find the creeks roaring with runoff and the lake level high. Other summers were marked by trickling streams, wider beaches and usually, the acrid smell and haze of smoke from a nearby forest fire.

The creek that meanders from Lily Lake, carving a sinuous path all the way to Fallen Leaf Lake, was one of the many constants I encountered in my summer respites. Like catching up with an old friend after a long separation, one of my rigid rituals upon arriving at Fallen Leaf Lake each year was to re-connect with Alpine Creek and follow its path from its headwaters to its delta.

High above Fallen Leaf lake, at the end of the paved road, waits a small and calm alpine lake—Lily Lake. There, melt waters from the snow packs gather from many of the valleys and peaks of Desolation Wilderness. Like a loving mother who sets a nutritious dinner, Lily Lake feeds Alpine Creek with a constant supply of fresh water. At the head of the creek, the icy clear waters spill over gently from the edge of Lily Lake. The rocks at the head of the creek and along its path are distinguished with sharp edges, poking up abruptly and haphazardly from the rushing water. Even the smaller stones along the banks are angular and sharp, as if cut abruptly by a wet saw.

The sound delights as flowing water ripples and gurgles away from Lily Lake and makes its way downstream. The current slows a bit and the creek becomes deeper and slower, creating perfect swimming and fishing holes. Beginning to gather momentum again, the water is drawn downward, as if anticipating a grand adventure ahead. Ripples and white water appear again as the creek continues its descent.

Moving, churning, and continuing to gather momentum, strength and speed, the creek suddenly and abruptly calms itself giving way to pools of water and slow moving current. Anticipation hangs in the air and one gets lost in the crystal-clear reflections of sky, trees, and endless beauty. But when one is truly present, another sound becomes more apparent and creeps into the forefront of the mind.

The roar. The roar of something unseen and mighty.

My eyes and ears are compelled to follow the sound through the tranquil stream pools to the water's edge. As if observing, the creek asks what lies beyond, and just as instantly, the water eagerly takes that final leap over time-smoothed stones to mingle with the thunderous power of Alpine Falls. Crashing and spraying against the huge boulders, the creek turns violent in this spot, cascading down to a set of stair-step rocks.

From my earliest memories, the Falls were the most magical part of the creek journey. The spray and power of the falls took my breath away and made me feel small, insignificant, yet connected to a vastness that made my legs weak. All surrounding distractions faded into nothingness as the falls, their roar, their majesty, their spray, commanded my entire attention. I can remember attempting to trace a single water drop as it began its descent over the edge of the falls, crashing, bouncing, and flying forcefully down the rocky cliffs. My eyes would strain to stay focused on the water drop as it mingled and merged with so many countless other drops on its journey.

At the base of the falls, the creek catches its breath and pauses in a small cove lined with wildflowers and pines. Making a final 90-degree turn, the creek becomes shallow and narrow again, easily rippling over rocks, determined to reach its destination. The roar from the falls becomes fainter until it has vanished completely. The creek murmurs quietly and gently as the water glides onward. Onward, consistently, quietly onward, flowing gently to the mouth of the Alpine Creek and Fallen Leaf Lake where the waters merge and become one.

Pebble to Ponder

Thoughts of the journey of the creek from Lily Lake to Fallen Leaf Lake still send chills up my spine. I long to trace the creek's path, to feel the awesome power of Alpine Falls, to hear the roar. I connect with the simplicity of the creek's journey, as well as the determined and confident way the creek makes its way through the forest to its destination. Boldly at times, roaring to be heard; at other moments, quietly flowing, merging effortlessly with the magnificent surroundings.

I am reminded of our journey through life and the ways in which our creeks run. Consider the simple message of this childhood song:

Row, row, row your boat,
Gently down the stream.
Merrily, merrily, merrily, merrily
Life is but a dream.

Our lives and work require consistent and persistent effort. We row, row, row our boat each day—working to complete a project, cook the evening meal, balance our checking accounts, and countless other projects that require rowing. Sometimes the rowing annoys us. We never seem to have enough time and we row our boats for hours, days, months, and years, wondering sometimes if we are really going anywhere. Stress and worry, strain, and sore muscles are side-effects of our rowing, but just like the creek that doesn't stop flowing, we keep rowing.

The trick, it seems to me, is in how we row. The trick is *gently down the stream*. Even in turbulent times when problems manifest themselves in the form of bouncing, white water that sprays and churns, we can choose to either row gently down the stream or to fight the current. If we fight the current, we wear ourselves out, make ourselves sick, and can become critical and grouchy. We spend all our energy in battle. The more we fight, the more we find we have to struggle, because to row upstream requires non-stop and aggressive rowing. By going with the flow, rowing gently, we conserve our strength so we can spend our energy appreciating the magnificent beauty and miracles that surround us. We appreciate the details, the little things that make up the everyday journeys of our lives.

Life is meant to be lived "Merrily, merrily, merrily, merrily." We get just one shot at life…our job is to find joy in the everyday business of rowing.

Alpine Creek travels merrily on its journey, focused on what it brings to the forest rather than what the forest owes it. The creek carries nourishing water and freely offers its gifts to animals, birds, fish, the plants and trees—and humans. The creek gives, and because its focus is on the giving, it travels *merrily*.

Going upward, walking along the road and following Alpine Creek back upstream to the shallow, wind-swept waters of Lily Lake, it's easy to believe *life is but a dream*. Destinations are often fuzzy and unclear when we begin to move toward them. Often all we have to go on is a vague feeling—a dream of what we will find on the other side of our "rowing."

Our lives are meant for reaching, for creating a better place, for dreaming. Without dreams, our rowing can seem pointless and without merit. Dreaming gives us permission to reinvent our lives every single day. Dreaming helps us discover our purpose, our unique gifts, that we can choose to offer up as effortlessly as Alpine Creek does to its surroundings. So ...

Row, row, row your boat
Gently down the stream.
Merrily, merrily, merrily, merrily
Life is but a dream.

In front of the store, Sheri, Diana, Dad, and nephew Jordan, ca 1994

PARTNERS
Telephone Poles

The key to success in life is
using the good thoughts of wise people.
—Leo Tolstoy

Road trips serve to replenish my spirit. The open road, a new delight just over the next hill, singing along with my favorite 1980s reject music when no one else can hear, fills me with a sense of calm and control. As long as I have detailed directions from point A to point B and decent weather conditions, road trips hold eager anticipation. Some drives may have fewer scenic highlights than others—like a business trip once I made from Sioux Falls and Pierre, South Dakota and then to Bismarck, North Dakota—but every road trip holds its delights and mysteries.

There's not much that can compare with the brilliant blue, clear sky of fall sharply contrasting with the golden fields of the Midwest plains that border the highway as far as you can see in every direction. This particular road trip boasted another punch of surprise color when I picked up the rental car and discovered I'd be driving through quaint country towns and America's heartland in a BRIGHT RED MUSTANG! (The Hertz Rental Car people told me they were out of the Buicks and would I mind driving the Mustang? I tried to act disappointed.)

On my way from Pierre to Bismarck, I zipped along a two-lane highway demarcated by twin lines of telephone poles. Towns and other signs of civilization were sparse and the telephone poles served to anchor me—people live where these telephone wires lead. The miles ticked slowly marked by milepost signs, an occasional billboard, and the telephone poles.

As I drove, I noticed a curious sight—the earth beneath one of the telephone poles had eroded away, leaving the pole suspended about 5 feet off the ground. My curiosity and need to stretch my aching legs led me to pull over to take a closer look. The anchorless pole continued to be held up by the poles on either side of it, as well as the wires connecting the whole system. Because the neighboring poles were firmly planted with strong foundations, the suspended pole looked as secure as all the others. The team of poles along the highway were all connected by the wires and thus, the suspended pole remained part of the team…receiving the same transmissions and contributing to the continuity and success of the chain of telephone poles winding through South Dakota.

After climbing back into my borrowed sports car and resuming my road trip my eyes occasionally wandered to the endless line of telephone poles. None I saw compared with the suspended pole, hanging silently in the air still making its contribution.

Pebble to Ponder

The lines of telephone poles stretching from one side of South Dakota to the other remind me of the importance of having partners in our lives. In business and in our personal lives, we seek teams with strong footings—a source of strength and support. We're connected to our teams by wires of common goals, good communication, and a mutual interpretation of what diverse events or actions mean for everyone on the team, within the network.

As leaders and managers, some wires include a well-founded focus on clear goals for sales, performance milestones, and deadlines. We all rely on the wires for feedback and guidance when challenges and unexpected detours occur.

With our partners we create more, accomplish more, and move our business forward with more strength by working together. We each bring a unique perspective to situations, challenges, and opportunities. By harnessing the power offered by those connecting wires of relationships, we are better able to see varying perspectives and increase the appeal and effectiveness our solutions have for the challenge at hand.

Surrounding ourselves with telephone poles that serve various functions in our lives is also a vital element in creating a strong network of connection. Imagine a long line of telephone poles connected to YOU and each within your reach. Some poles include your parents, siblings, your spouse/life partner. Other poles may be a business coach, a health and fitness expert, your financial advisor, your spiritual connection, or perhaps a professional networking group. Understanding the connection of excellent partnerships gives us shortcuts when difficult or new challenges present themselves— there are others who are firmly rooted in solid ground, experts in an area where we seek wisdom. By *using the good thoughts of wise people,* as Leo Tolstoy stated, we find greater success more often than when we attempt to transmit our messages all alone.

Sometimes, too, we find ourselves suspended or supported by the efforts of our partners—our team, our family, our network of friends. We gain strength, stability, and connection and are held firmly in place even when the earth has eroded beneath us and we sway a bit in the prairie winds.

Reach out to some of the key *telephone poles* around you this week and strengthen the special power of those relationships.

Give back to your partners by maintaining your strong footing so when needed, you can support the one swinging in the wind.

PEACE
Eventide

*In our joy, we think we hear a whisper. We listen carefully as it
gathers strength. We hear a sweetness. The word is peace.*
—Maya Angelou

Each afternoon at Sherman Cabin, my sister and I could be found on our private swim dock. Mom had two rules when it came to how Diana and I spent our vacation time: 1) wait 20 minutes after eating before getting in the water, and 2) we could be in the water only during the hours that sunshine covered the dock. Peering down at the dock from the corner of the cabin's wrap-around porch, we became expert at predicting exactly when the sun's angle would bathe our dock in its warm rays.

Wooden planks, some in better condition than others, formed our narrow L-shaped afternoon base. The dock was so narrow that we could line up beach towels single file to give us protection from the weather-worn wood. Here we spent hours every day splashing, swimming, sunning—basically letting the time flow by languidly. Water games, paddle boat rides, inner tube races, or peering through the icy clear water with swim masks for treasures became our rituals.

Our only connection to the passage of time was the movement of the sun as it crossed high overhead and made its slow and steady descent toward Mount Cathedral. In the late afternoon, sunlight would sparkle on the water, making the lake come alive with a shimmering blanket of diamonds. This was the ideal time to be in the water as the extra burst of sunlight warmed our backs, dried our towels, and heated the surface of the lake.

Continuing its descent, the great sun moved implacably toward Mount Cathedral in their daily appointment that cast the far side of the lake into deep shadow, alerting us to the last hours of watery pleasure. When at last the two mighty icons appeared to touch, the back side of Mount Cathedral and the peaks and valleys of Desolation Wilderness became bathed in brightness. Each day, this was our signal to leave our play behind, tie up the inner tubes and take ourselves back up the hill to the smells and tastes of dinner and the laughter of evening games.

Eventide—my favorite time of day at Fallen Leaf Lake. Sometimes, I'd linger on the dock and watch the sun finish its journey behind the purple-gray rock and pine covered mountain. Other days, I'd watch the sky for an hour or more after the great sun's exit and marvel at the changing mood and color of the heavens and how those changes reflected on the water. At dusk one particular day, when I was about 14, I felt inspired to write the following:

> *I gaze at the shadows in the trees*
> *As the sun glides slowly, but with ease*
> *And there's really nothing I would rather do*
> *Than to watch the sky change from pink, to purple to blue.*

The sun has gone behind the mountain,
And the shadows slowly fade.
The once white puffs of cloud are now faintly turning pink
And the purple in the background, makes me stop to think:
How small I am in this never ending space
And can I stand the wait to see the Creator's face?

I gaze at the shadows in the sky
And wish I could gain wings and fly!
And there's really nothing I would rather do
Than to watch the sky change from pink, to purple to blue.

Pebble to Ponder

In defining peace, the dictionary uses words like "mutual harmony, freedom from anxiety, tranquility, and serenity." Finding such peace in our chaotic world is often a low priority when we're faced with the demands of each day. There is simply too much to be done and too little time in which to do it.

Corporations deem productive employees as the ones who can accomplish the work of two or three people without complaint of compromise in quality. We rise, exercise, work, worship, support our children's activities, and retire each night, only to begin the cycle again in only a few short hours. The quest for peace is often elusive.

Yet making time and place for mutual harmony and freedom from anxiety feeds our souls in ways that are poorly described in words. Even as a young teen, sitting in silence to watch the sun set behind a beloved mountain filled my heart with peace. Watching the sky change from pink to purple to blue connected me in harmony with my family, my dreams, my hopes, and my world at the tender age of 14 . Finding the same connection today takes more effort and planning.

Or does it? Perhaps sitting quietly in the back garden listening to the chorus of chickadees and robins on a warm July afternoon can be just as connecting. Or being moved by a violin soloist playing *Amazing Grace*. Or looking up at a clear October night full of stars. Or reading a description of perfect beauty. Perhaps peace is all around us, inviting us to reach out and embrace it.

The restoring stillness of Lily Lake.

PRESSURE
Garden Hoses

Imperfect action is better than perfect inaction.
—Harry Truman

Summer is without a doubt my favorite season. I LIVE all year for the long afternoons, evenings, the smell of dinner cooking on the BBQ, the sunshine, and the need to give my flower garden some extra water with the garden hose. I have one of those fun little nozzles on the end of my backyard hose—the kind that when you squeeze on the handle, the water comes out in an even shower. When you let go of the handle, the valve in the nozzle shuts and holds the water back without you having to turn the water off at the source—a pretty handy gadget!

Garden hoses are not without frustrating challenges, however. A while back, I grew tired of rolling up my hose every time I finished watering the yard—so I purchased an innovative contraption that looks like a ceramic pot and is designed to keep my hose hidden from view. To conceal my hose neatly in my new ceramic pot, I first needed to unroll the hose and re-roll it inside the pot. After a long winter of idleness, my garden hose was full of bends and kinks and twists. The painstaking process of unbending the long, green, snakelike tool and then forcing it to bend and lay optimally in the decorative pot took more time than I anticipated. My efforts, however, yielded more than an aesthetic result. Once re-rolled inside the container, I was amazed to find the water pressure from the garden hose had increased dramatically. The next afternoon when I pulled the hose from the ceramic pot, water flowed freely without kinks to my plants and garden!

Sometimes water pressure is not what is needed to best nourish the plants in my yard. Our side-yard is a hot and sunny location during the dry Seattle summer. Even with my longest, 100-foot-long garden hose, reaching all the plants with needed water is impossible. When using the high-pressure setting on my garden hose nozzle, the water would often skip across the baked, dry ground and travel right down the storm drain. Carrying water to the plants in the side yard with watering cans took too much time and patience, not to mention strength.

So, I sought the experts at the garden nursery. They suggested a soaker hose as a way to both conserve water and reduce the amount of water pressure needed to keep the side-yard plants hydrated. I carefully snaked the soaker hose around all the plants in the side-yard and buried the soaker hose just under the surface of the soil. Leaving the nozzle at the end exposed, I connected the permanently installed soaker hose to my garden hose. Now instead of great streams of water hitting the plants and washing away the earth at the surface, the soaker hose allowed hundreds of small drips to percolate into the soil surrounding the plants. Even on the hottest summer days, the soaker hose effectively provides water to my side-yard landscape.

Pebble to Ponder

When we are closed off to what is possible, when we harbor doubt, fear, and negativity ("it will never work"), we are just like my garden hose nozzle holding back every drop of nourishing, life-giving water we carry within us! It's only when we believe and open our valves through positive thoughts, soaring attitudes, and patient, persistent actions that we begin to attract success. As we let water flow freely from our garden hose nozzles, we nourish our lives, our families, our business endeavors, and our gardens are healthy and magnificent!

Most certainly, we all encounter kinks, bends, and twists in our lives that when discovered and unbent, would provide more PRESSURE, more energy, more enthusiasm. How would more water pressure serve your efficiency and success? How can opening ourselves to flow freely allow us to work less hard … and more smart? Find those kinks, and … well … unbend them! Seek out new ways to increase your water pressure.

Sometimes a soaker hose is a better approach to nourishing our mental gardens. Have you ever felt so baked and dry from the demands of your day that any attempt at nourishment would just run off and travel down the storm drain? To allow nourishment to penetrate, sink in and do its job when we are baked dry from stress is to let little drops of water soak into our minds. This might be accomplished by using a place of personal retreat where we can be still and let time slip slowly by, allowing the consistent presence of dripping water soften our baked, dry ground. Once cooled and refreshed by the persistent drops of motivational water, we are better able to face the baking demands of our lives.

The old Store at Fallen Leaf Lake Lodge

PROSPERITY
Stores

The price of anything is the amount of life you exchange for it.
—Henry David Thoreau

The heart of Fallen Leaf Lodge sat centered at the south end of the lake, strong and secure within feet of the crystal-clear water. Its simple sign conveyed in one word to any visitor or resident the essential nature of its purpose: Store. The all-wood building matched the other buildings at the Lodge with brown painted siding and forest-green trim around the windows and doors. While not at all modern, The Store possessed a magic and charm that I doubt could be duplicated or recreated anywhere.

From lakeside, entering The Store required climbing a set of wide, wooden stairs that creaked and moaned in the same places year after year. The staircase emptied onto a wrap-around porch that served multiple purposes—not only did it offer one of the best picture-snapping views of the lake, it was a great place for parents to keep an eye on their children wading in the water at the beach just across the street, and also housed several notice boards for happenings at the lake and important messages from the Forest

Service. A rickety, wooden screen door served as the only public entrance into The Store and the familiar sound of the door slamming shut with its rusty spring behind every patron became a low-tech security way for the staff to stay abreast of people coming and going.

Inside, The Store's well-organized array of supplies, food stuffs and treats catered to the anticipated needs of campers, residents, and day-trippers to Fallen Leaf Lodge. I loved to walk slowly up and down each aisle, marveling at the variety and creativity of the items contained on each shelf, attempting to spot new arrivals as I browsed. While the wooden shelves always appeared well stocked, the quantities of each item was carefully managed to ensure adequate room for all the other items competing for attention in the quaint and compact space. Everything a camping family could need to complete their rations or replace a forgotten item could be found among the treasures of the store. Jiffy-Pop® popcorn, mini-ketchup and mustard bottles, salt, matches, paper plates, and corn bread mix seemed to be among the more popular supplies. For the outdoor enthusiasts, fishing gear and live bait, swim/beach toys, canteens, pocket knives, and bird books lined one entire wall.

Each year, new Fallen Leaf Lake gear—hats, T-shirts, sweatshirts, and jackets were displayed in new colors and designs. A small freezer and refrigerated section held ice and beverages and a moderate quantity of fresh meat and produce that arrived by truck only a couple of times a week. Near the cash register stood an old-fashioned ice cream freezer that kept the most colorful and flavorful assortment of popsicles and ice cream treats I had ever seen in one place.

The Store always buzzed with activity, and as the heart of the Fallen Leaf Lodge, became a place where camping neighbors and full-time residents met spontaneously to shoot the breeze, or discuss the size of the fish caught that morning, or the weather, or the best hikes. The college students who rang up sales, kept the floors swept, and the freezer stocked were my heroes—I dreamed of growing up and working in The Store... just like them.

My sister and I mimicked our enviable future jobs by creating our own pretend version of The Store along Alpine Creek near the campground. I always played the shop -keeping college student and Diana always played the customers. We set up our mock assortment of camping rations on a rock formation that lined the creek; it only took a bit of imagination to see how well it resembled shelves. We even created an entrance to our store along a narrow strip of rocks that joined together to create a natural stairway leading up from the bank of the creek along the side of our rock formation.

Our shelves were stocked with an assortment of bark and pinecones and a few small toys smuggled from our stash at camp. We pretended the bark was ice cream or food and the pinecones, depending on their size, were designated as boxes of cereal or bait for fish. Sticks and branches became fishing poles and whisk brooms. On days it wasn't needed for transporting ice, we'd borrow Dad's canvas shopping bag to use for the collected mock groceries. When it came time to pay, Diana pulled out leaves of assorted sizes and shapes that we had designated various monetary denominations. The goal of our game was clear—to solve any supply problem by having just THE thing on hand in our store by the creek.

Pebble to Ponder

The Store at Fallen Leaf Lodge bore tribute to the principles of abundance, prosperity, and sometimes, scarcity. As a young patron of The Store, observing these principles manifest were occasionally difficult for me to grasp—especially when it came to scarcity.

Properly anticipating the needs of the customers clearly played a vital role in running a smooth operation and in the seasonal success of The Store. I noticed items disappearing from both over- and under-selling. Items that didn't sell well and those that were in high demand didn't linger long in The Store's inventory. On the days of the week when the ice blocks arrived, needy campers converged at The Store within moments, eager to replenish their food chests with needed refrigeration. While it didn't happen often, sometimes my favorite ice cream treat would be missing from the freezer. By August each year, the selection of colors and sizes of Fallen Leaf gear waned, and the shelves that held the coveted apparel appeared lonely. I recall how one year, a low-calorie pancake mix on the shelf didn't sell well (in the days before we worried about low-calorie food options); one day that summer, one of my college student heroes sat on the floor replacing the low-calorie mix with the correct FULL-calorie version to encourage more sales.

Once we were old enough to be trusted to mind the traffic, Diana and I were often sent to The Store with a short list of necessities, the canvas grocery bag, and a ten-dollar bill. Dad had become a master at understanding the forces of supply and demand at The Store and often sent us with several "Plan B" items in case his first choice wasn't available. Even so, during those peak summer vacation weeks, we'd often return to Sherman Cabin with a half-empty grocery bag and disappointed looks when The Store had run out of the things we'd been sent to fetch.

Abundance and scarcity show up in our lives in various ways, some much more subtly than stock on hand at a country store. I've found that both abundance and scarcity operate on the *ripple principle*. It takes only a single drop of abundance in the pond of our life to ripple outward and create more abundance. Additionally, the more we focus on abundance, the more abundance we experience, and like fire feeding fire, the flames of prosperity and success grow brighter and hotter, presenting us with even more opportunities for abundance.

The reverse also seems to hold true. When we exist in a pattern of negativity and scarcity, that pattern also tends to ripple outward and create more negativity and scarcity.

I'm not proposing that the ripple principle is the cause for every period of abundance or scarcity in our lives. Certainly, unexpected events and tragedies happen that can halt a ripple of prosperity instantly. A sudden miraculous event can also trigger abundance where only negativity and scarcity existed before.

To keep our stores operating in an environment of prosperity and abundance, the challenge is to anticipate the needs of those we serve and to be able to provide "just THE thing" when it is needed. When we live from a place of abundance—believing there will always be enough of what we need—enough pancake mix, enough ice blocks, and the very size and color T-shirt we were hoping for—we are much more likely to experience prosperity more fully.

One step at a time!

PERSISTENCE
50-Yard Dash

Perseverance is not a long race; it is many short races,
one after another.
—Walter Elliott

In my elementary school years, I was the one last to be picked for relay races and the 50-yard dash. My young schoolmates knew something about me that I did not see for many years—I ran TO the finish line, and not THROUGH the finish line. When my turn to dash came up, I'd give it everything my little legs could offer and run with all my heart. At the starting whistle, I'd typically be near the front of the pack as we all sprinted toward the goal. As soon as my eyes glimpsed the finish line painted on the blacktop, however, I'd begin to slow down. By the time I reached the finish line, my sprint had slowed to a stroll. Needless to say, I don't have any certificates of excellence in my scrapbook for track and field!

Basically, I am a spectator when it comes to races and dashes. From watching the Olympic track-and-field events to participating in a parent cheering section at my kids' school track meets, the perseverance needed to run a race fascinates me. Like the quote from Walter Elliott, a race is really divided up into many "short races, one after another." Track involves as much mental preparation as physical conditioning.

Today I share my home with a determined, young athlete—my son, Alex. Alex is a natural when it comes to sports, and track and field is among his specialties. Alex runs THROUGH the finish line and approaches each race with an intense desire to win. During practice and at meets, he is keenly focused on improving his time on the 100-meter and relay races. And while his time decreases in very small increments, he is driven by the possibility of a faster performance with each attempt. He is consistent, patient, and persistent in his practice routines and habits. He stretches and warms up prior to each race. He walks the length of the track and practices his start from the blocks. He wears the right shoes, his lucky T-shirt, and makes certain he has a full breakfast before he even steps foot on the track.

I also observe the mental preparation Alex and his fellow track teammates go through. Long before they are called to line up in the starting blocks, the relay team is seen on the grassy mid-field practicing their baton hand-offs. They talk to each other, pump each other up, or stretch and sit silently listening to a favorite tune on their iPod. They visualize every aspect of the race, from the starting gun to the finish line. They picture themselves running through the finish line.

Pebble to Ponder

To better run the race of our lives, our challenge is to run THROUGH the finish line—believing we have the skills and tools to run the race. Anytime we strive toward a goal or a finish line in our lives, it's important to celebrate the successes we make along the way—each time we shave a second or two off our best race time.

On his 90th birthday, historical figure and member of the U.S. Supreme Court for over fifty years, Oliver Wendell Holmes, had this to say about races:

> *The riders in a race do not stop short when they reach the goal.*
> *There is a little finishing canter before coming to a standstill.*
> *There is time to hear the kind voices of friends and to say to*
> *oneself: The work is done. But just as one says that, the answer*
> *comes: "The race is over, but the work is never done while the*
> *power to work remains. For to live is to function.*
> *That is all there is to living.*
> —Radio address given by Oliver Wendell Holmes, March 7, 1931

Being persistent in our practice routines and habits also serves us as we race. The *American Heritage Dictionary* defines persistent in two interesting ways: 1) refusing to give up or let go; 2) insistently repetitive or continuous. By believing in the possibility of winning, by being consistent and patient with ourselves … and remembering to eat a full breakfast before we even step foot on the track, we will run a successful race.

Enjoy running with the wind blowing through your hair, and remember to keep running, as fast as your little legs can carry you, all the way THROUGH the finish line.

Conquering the Mighty Truckee River

PIONEERING
Truckee River

*The real voyage of discovery consists not in seeking new
landscapes, but in having new eyes.*
—Marcel Proust

Countless streams, rivers and waterfalls flow throughout the magnificent Sierra Nevada Mountains. Filled from melting snow and ice, these waterways carry water from the mountain peaks down to the valleys and eventually to the lakes and communities that surround Lake Tahoe. One of the best known rivers is the Truckee River, a 140-mile-long tributary that originates in the snow packs near Pyramid Lake and carries water to the Lake Tahoe area through Tahoe City and Truckee, California, all the way down to Sparks, Reno, and Carson City, Nevada. In addition to adding to the water supply for these communities and serving as home to fish, the Truckee River is widely used for recreation, including river rafting. In search of a new adventure one year in my late teens, my family ventured to Tahoe City to check out the options for a day on the Truckee.

It had been a particularly dry year and an extremely hot summer, so the water levels of the streams and lakes were much lower than normal. Even though we left Sherman Cabin early, right after breakfast, we could tell the day was going to be a scorcher—well into the mid 80s. Diana and I were excited to try something new, while Mom and Dad chattered with family friends, Bob and Barbara Sanders, who were joining us for a few days of our vacation. Our entourage was completed with the yippy presence of Charlie, our tan teacup poodle, who panted in his bed in the front seat of our Suburban.

Bob and Barbara Sanders are our oldest family friends. Barbara car-pooled with Mom when they both worked in Oakland, and Dad and Bob were "brothers" in the Concord Elks Club. The four of them regularly double-dated before Mom and Dad where married and the couple served as witnesses at my parents' wedding.

The Sanders, from my young perspective, made an interesting pair and always seemed to me to be very much in love. Barbara had been born and raised in England and moved to the States after meeting Bob, who was stationed in London at the U.S. Air Force base. Bob comes from Mississippi. So just listening to the two of them was fascinating, as Bob's southern drawl played off Barbara's refined vowels. They were always taking care of each other. Barbara made Bob's coffee every day, and Bob always offered his arm when they walked. He also opened every door for his wife. What's more, they always called each other "Love."

After the long and winding drive from Fallen Leaf on Highway 89 through Emerald Bay, Meeks Bay, and Tahoe City, and after singing to the country western classics of Willie Nelson and Loretta Lynn, we arrived at a wide spot off the road where the edge of the highway met a flat gravel lined wayside where a hand-painted sign boasted the "best Truckee River floating." The marketing of the floating experience left a little to be desired. A couple of trailer trucks were stacked high with inflated river rafts. A couple of guys stood near the trailers handing out release forms and oars for everyone thinking about making the river journey. A small brown, rickety card table held an empty soup can of those little mini-pencils (like the kind you use when you play miniature golf), and a taped sign "ALL RAFTING DONE AT OWN RISK" completed the registration area.

We each dutifully completed our release forms, and handed them to one of the raft guys. The discussion that followed is fuzzy in my memory, but the outcome demonstrates my father's honed skill of "getting out of something he didn't want to do and making it look like the very best option possible with no one being upset after." Dogs were not allowed in the rafts, and because the day was shaping up to be so hot, we did not want to leave little Charlie in the car while we paddled down the river—meaning someone would have to stay behind with the dog. Mom volunteered first to do the dog-sitting.

It was Dad who won out, saying that the rafting would be bad for his back, plus he would sweeten the deal by driving our car down to the end point of the tour so we wouldn't have to pile into the courtesy shuttle after we were all wet and tired. We all knew Mom would probably get lost trying to follow the river, and we couldn't argue that the bumpy ride might be painful for Dad's chronic back condition. Ultimately, everyone agreed that Dad's plan was magnificent, and oars in hand, the rest of us marched down to the river bank to conquer the mighty Truckee.

Our first, and what looked like a simple task, was to climb into the raft and claim a corner from which to paddle. Without Dad, our group consisted of five passengers so we decided to spread ourselves out with one in the front of the raft, two in the middle, and two on the back end. I opted for one of the back end positions with Bob, while

Diana and Barbara ended up in the middle, leaving Mom in front. The laughter and giggling that accompanied the boarding of our water craft carried high above the trees and the din of the highway noise. Mom wasn't known for her balance, so it was decided she should be the first to climb into the raft so if it went over, she'd be the only one getting wet.

The first step is always the worst. Grasping one of the raft guys with one hand and her oar with the other, Mom stepped down and her feet and legs began to dance around the soft bottom of the boat. She swayed and "ooooooohed" and the boat splashed until she finally landed on her backside at the front of the raft.

Eventually, laughing and giggling until our sides hurt and our jaws ached, all five of us managed to board the raft. With a wave, a ceremonial photo opportunity, and a call of "Good Luck," the raft guys pushed us out into the gentle current.

It took a few minutes to practice the art of the oars and to synchronize our paddling so the raft moved downriver rather than in circles. At the back end of the raft, I discovered I had a lot of steering control. In fact, when Mom and Barbara stopped rowing in front to point out a tree or family of ducks, we would begin to circle toward the left. The refrain still rings in my ears: "Paddle, Sheri, paddle! Paddle, Sheri, paddle," as only Bob could say it in his thick southern drawl, having appointed himself captain of our craft.

We soon mastered (well, sort of) the art of rowing in unison and began gliding down the Truckee River with ease. The current was very tame and the water quite shallow. Parts of the river were neatly divided into two streams with sand and pebbles and brush growing in the center where the water had receded. The late morning sun grew hotter and we reapplied our waterproof sunscreen and nibbled on nectarines. Lake Tahoe water is known to be among the purest in the world, so we reasoned the crystal clear and delightfully cool river water was safe to drink and drank freely from the river to stay hydrated.

At one point, the river's current lacked the strength to propel us forward, so Bob instructed me to climb out of the raft and pull us along to deeper water. The cool water felt exhilarating on my legs, and everyone welcomed the break from their oars while I guided us manually. I pulled the raft as the water gradually became deeper. All of a sudden, the river bottom dropped out from below my feet and I was swimming. At the same time, the river current began to accelerate and I found it difficult to keep up with the raft.

"BOB! I can't catch up! Pull over to the side so I can climb back in!" I called to our captain.

Bob instantly put the rest of the crew to work: "Paddle, Shirley, paddle… Paddle, Barbara, paddle…" While it took a little time to navigate sideways, Bob successfully parked the raft, I swam to it and pulled myself up over the side and back into our barge. I heard familiar, yet distant laughter, and looking up the bank, saw Dad smiling and laughing and waving at us from the safety of higher ground. He was following our journey from above.

After my swim, the river float became easy again, and I began to wonder why the men had wished us "good luck" and why the sign had said "ALL RAFTING DONE AT OWN RISK." We must be naturals, I decided, as nothing had been difficult or treacherous on this watery adventure as yet. Sure, the water was a little deeper now, and the current was carrying us faster downstream, but it was nothing we couldn't handle.

Clarity comes in interesting ways.

Suddenly, the mighty Truckee River ceased to be calm and smooth and began to show gurgling ripples of white, churning water flowing fast and hard over rocks. Suddenly, we were spinning in circles again, as Bob's chant grew louder and more intense: "PADDLE, SHERI, PADDLE!!! PADDLE, SHERI, PADDLE!!!" I switched into auto pilot and began to paddle without regard of what Mom and Barbara were doing in front—I just needed to get us pointed in the right direction again!

"OUCH!" Mom exclaimed as we hit a rock that bounced under the raft and grazed the backsides of her legs with unforgiving hardness.

"HEY!" Diana cried out, thinking I had splashed her with oar water when in fact the rapids had kicked water up and over the raft and hit her square in the face.

"PADDLE, SHERI…. PADDLE SHERI… PADDLE, PADDLE!!!"

Splash! Bounce! Splash!

"OUCH! Oh, geez!"

"PADDLE SHERI, PADDLE!"

"BOB! Look at that—are we going OVER that?"

Just about twenty feet ahead, the river dropped over a squatty waterfall and emptied into calmer, quiet waters again, demarcating the exit point for our rafting adventure. There was no going back. The river was moving too swiftly to turn toward the shore. Diana was crying. Mom was worried. Barbara was paddling faster. Bob was chanting louder. And I knew the only way out was over the drop to the waiting raft guys. I glanced around to get my bearings and help determine the best way over, when I caught glimpse of my father standing near the exit dock, laughing in hysterics. And briefly, because there really wasn't much time to think, I stammered "Why didn't I VOLUNTEER to stay with Charlie?"

"PADDLE, SHERI!!! FASTER, FASTER… PADDLE SHERI!"

Whoosh.

And then it was done. We glided to the dock and the raft guys without even a single stroke of our oars. The life vests came off, we climbed over each other to get out of our bouncy orange raft, and ate lunch at a café overlooking the waterfall we had tumbled over, telling Dad all about our brave adventure. We had conquered the mighty Truckee River.

Pebble to Ponder

Ah, to be a pioneer. To be first to see what lies around the next bend of the river or on the other side of the mountain. To be the first to taste, the first to smell, the first to touch the undiscovered. I'm certain there must be an excitement and exhilaration like no other when your wagon is the first to enter the valley.

To create a homestead beautiful and lasting from barren prairie. To spend a lifetime searching for a place to call home. To invest your time and soul and all your energy to create a town and community that works together for the common good. To spearhead exploration. To "boldly go where no one has gone before." While their lives were difficult and filled with danger and uncertainty, my pioneer roots call to me every now and then and beckon me to BE more pioneering.

My childhood adventure down the mighty Truckee River taught me a few lessons about being pioneering. To BE pioneering means more than wearing a bonnet or planting corn. It's more about curiosity and fortitude and leadership. Despite our creature comforts and technology, and regardless of our roles in career and home, BEING pioneering can help us conquer any river life presents us. Consider these characteristics of a pioneer.

A pioneer is an explorer who is eager to see what might be, or what we haven't found. We begin our lives open to exploring, and along the way, if we aren't careful, we decide that being methodical and predictable are better. Pioneers search. Pioneers explore just for the sake of expanding their perspective.

A pioneer is a pathfinder, a decision-maker. To take the left or right fork in the river? To blaze a new trail or take the one trodden in the wood? A pioneer finds the path that best leads to the desired destination. Sometimes that means venturing ahead to scout out each path before settling on the best one. What obstacles and dangers lie ahead? What resources can we best make use of on our journey? Pioneers create paths.

A pioneer is a creator. Pioneers are always adding to their bags of tricks and solutions to tricky situations. Creating a way of gathering water along the river, or feeding the family with nectarines utilize creativity to ensure success. A pioneer is willing to do something completely new.

A pioneer is a contributor. Pioneers don't act alone and instead embrace the notion that many hands make light work. One person at the oars in our raft would have made for a difficult and long journey, but with five of us, each contributing our strength and focus toward our goal of conquering the river, we prevailed. Pioneers improve on what works. Always wanting to improve the quality and efficiency of the journey, pioneers look for innovative combinations of solutions. On the river, we discovered it was easier to maintain a straight course down the river when Bob kept his oar in the water, acting like a rudder, while I paddled.

Ah, to be a pioneer!

POWER
Triathlon

Whatever you can do, or believe you can do, begin it.
For boldness has genius, power and magic in it.
—Goethe

W ho can ignore the barrage of messages inviting us to live a healthy lifestyle, to be physically fit, and maintain an ideal weight? Our adult lifestyles often include routines that don't lend themselves to regular physical activity, and thus has spawned a lucrative industry—that of the health club. The sights and smells of the typical health club have never really appealed to me, so when an all-women boutique fitness center opened in Maple Valley, I decided to join.

With the enthusiasm of a NEW goal, I set out a rigorous schedule of five cardio and three resistance circuit training sessions per week, and was beginning to feel stronger and fitter with each passing day. One spring morning, one of the owners approached me while I was counting up to my set of 15 repetitions on the bench press.

"I'm going to sponsor a mini-triathlon this summer—you should do it!" She must have caught me in a moment of oxygen deprivation, because after asking what the mini-triathlon included (a ¼ mile swim, followed by a 14.2-mile bike ride, and finishing with a 3-mile run) I answered: "Sure, sounds like fun!"

Since it was only March, and the event wasn't scheduled until late July, I felt reasonably confident I could be ready to tackle this tribute to fitness. The inner critic in my head whispered: "Are you crazy? Do you really think YOU can do a triathlon?"

The following Saturday, I dug through the garage to locate my bike helmet and bike that had been gathering dust. I sent the bike in for a tune up and had a speedometer installed so I could track the length of my rides. Next, I sought out a pair of running shoes, and the padded stretchy shorts that make bike riding a little more comfortable. As an extra measure of commitment, I joined Weight Watchers and started counting my daily intake, weighing in weekly, and cutting out my favorite pasta with cream sauce dishes.

Spring melted into early summer and I felt pleased with my progress on my bike. On average, I was logging five or six rides of between 12-20 miles each per week. I smiled every time I mounted my bike, and my rides became therapeutic—a time to disconnect the day's demands and listen to the birds as I followed the path along Cedar River from Maple Valley to Renton.

I turned my attention to running in early June. Unlike the biking portion, running did not put a smile on my face. I found it torturous and boring, and hard on my hips and knees. After nearly three weeks, I had only managed to get up to a mile before stopping. A work colleague suggested I work at going the full three miles, walking as much as I needed to, then gradually building up the time that I ran. By late June, I was combining biking and running, with a few lap swims added for good measure.

By July 1st, just three weeks before the big event, I felt fairly confident I might actually be strong enough to do this crazy thing!

My rehearsal and preparation included significant visualization as the days clicked by. As I ran, I imagined myself crossing the finish line, and unlike the poor performance of my youth in the 50-yard dash, I imagined myself running across the finish line with a last burst of speed and momentum. I planned my after-event reward— a tasty tortellini with cream sauce and prosciutto and fresh peas from a favorite Italian restaurant, visualizing its buttery taste. I prepared my event snacks, practiced my wardrobe changes, and watched long-range weather forecasts to prepare for event-day climate conditions.

Three days prior to the scheduled event, I received a phone call that threw my enthusiasm into turmoil. Due to issues involving permits, permission from the city, and misinformation from the partner who was co-sponsoring the event with my fitness center, the triathlon would be postponed to an unknown date in the fall. My heart sank. The finish line and accomplishment that lay only a few days away had been diverted. My enthusiasm, dedication, and commitment suffered and I took a holiday from my intense training. My running shoes sat on a shelf, and my biking frequency slowed to a few rides a week through the summer heat of August.

A second phone call came the week before Labor Day. The Triathlon was back on again, set for the third week of September. Knowing I had lost some endurance— especially in the running portion—I battled with myself on whether to participate. Could I be ready again in such a short time? What if the weather turned sour and the event was cancelled again? Should I just wait and participate the following summer instead? These arguments, however, paled in comparison to the visual image of crossing the finish line, of reaching a goal that had seemed so out of reach in the spring. Somewhere deep inside I knew I needed to see this through—to prove to myself I could run this race.

I rose on the morning of September 17 before any evidence of daylight. The forecast called for steady rain and cool temperatures. Butterflies fluttered in my tummy as I loaded up my bike and duffle bag filled with needed supplies. It was time to trust in the months of preparation and focus on completing the task. I sat at my breakfast bar, fueling up for the morning with a tall glass of cold milk and a pile of scrambled eggs sprinkled with grated cheddar.

As I ate, I considered the importance of FUEL before any journey. In life, business, and when running a triathlon, FUEL comprises all the preparation, training, and mental rehearsal that culminate in the anticipation of an amazing accomplishment. The start of each new day, in fact, is an opportunity to FUEL up, to rehearse how we want the day to unfold, consider solutions to problems that await us at the office, or visualize an outstanding result on a school exam.

We FUEL our goals through mental rehearsal, anticipating that despite the weather forecast or other obstacles, today has the potential to be our best day ever. The point of power always lies in the present moment.

Pebble to Ponder
FOUR Questions to Claim Personal Power

1. **What?** When I arrived at the designated starting area about 6:00 a.m., pre-race activities were well underway. I was met by a race coordinator, who instructed me on forms to complete and where to report to be officially checked-in. I received my official race number and was given an identification sign to mount on my bicycle and running

shirt. Additionally, with the aid of a sharpie marker, my number was drawn on one arm, one leg and atop my head on the requisite lime-green swim cap. Finally, I was issued an ankle strap that would monitor my time for each event, as well as total time for the race. After being completely identified as #14, I was instructed to complete my preparations in a roped-off staging area. I carefully laid out the clothing, towels, running shoes, and snacks I would need between events.

At last, with everything in order, I reported for the official start of the triathlon on the muddy shores of Lake Wilderness for the ¼-mile swim.

Preparation of our staging area in any endeavor in life or business is a key step in claiming our personal power. We accomplish goals more swiftly, meet objectives and corporate deadlines with more regularity when we have prepared our staging area. While it may appear to a passerby that we are scurrying around without purpose, ensuring that our plans, our supplies, our resources are lined up in the order we will use them, is as important a component as the actual race (project or task).

Good old-fashioned organization sets us up to be successful with awareness of WHAT is needed and proactively setting appointments on our calendar rather than letting the day happen to us. This is race strategy at the basic level—WHAT do I need to complete my race, and how will I prepare it so it is accessible when I need it?

2. *Gut?* The sound of the starting gun pierced through my anticipation and my legs began to carry me forward with the throng of other participants into the cold and murky water of Lake Wilderness. Without the luxury of slow acclimation to the water temperature, I charged forward to a depth that allowed me to kick off the squidgy lake bottom and begin to swim. A simple rhythm began to emerge: kick, stroke, breathe, kick, stroke

breathe and I soon forgot about the cold water. Cheers from the shore faded completely as we swam to a small boat and floating marker that marked our half-way point. My focus became laser-sharp as my co-competitors splashed and passed me on our swim: kick, stroke, breath, kick, stroke, breathe. I slowly became aware of the sounds from the shore again as my strokes carried me to more shallow water and finally to a depth where my feet scraped the lake bottom.

Standing and running toward the shore and staging area my GUT began to speak to me—"One event down, two to go—still so FAR from the finish and already I'm tired." I pushed the thoughts down as the cold air met my dripping body. I peeled off my swim cap, and prepared for the bike ride.

Our GUT has a way of reminding us of emotional connection and feeling as we run our race. Our gut can serve us by connecting us to our reason—our why, our purpose in our pursuit. The butterflies, anticipation, and adrenaline we feel as we find our rhythm can help us keep sharp focus. A more critical voice in our GUT can also emerge, and unless we are aware of its message, can derail, discourage, and distract us from our focus.

Claiming our personal power includes awareness of our GUT messages. How am I feeling? Is this emotion serving and supporting my goals and objectives, or is it attempting to derail my purpose and sabotage my focus?

3. *So What?* I knew going into the triathlon that the bike portion would be my favorite and most successful segment. By working from this strength, I would make up some time lost in my slow and steady swim, re-gain strength reserves in anticipation of the run, and enjoy the ride with the wind in my face. It was time to put my head down and fall into the familiar rhythm. One of the event's rules prohibited the use of mp3 players,

so my companion iPod present on every training ride was absent. I had created a play list called "14.2 miles" that included exactly the number of songs it would typically take me to ride 14.2 miles. I used it in my training to pace myself and to help pass the time on days I felt less motivated to pedal.

Without the iPod and even though a few co-competitors were nearby, I opted to sing my play list anyway. Watching the odometer and singing my tunes as I raced helped keep me connected to how far I'd come and how far I still had to go. I knew that with each push-pull of my bike pedal, I was one moment closer to the finish line. As Lake Wilderness Park and the race staging area came into view, I burst into a satisfied smile. While mental rehearsal had prepared me for the possibility of finishing the triathlon, the moment I dismounted my bike, I believed completely, without doubt I would finish.

"SO WHAT" is our connection to the mini-wins and benchmarks that make up each goal or dream we set off to accomplish. Benchmarks are important to keep us on pace toward our goals. With the passing of each moment, hour and day, we are either making progress toward our goals, standing still, or losing momentum. Knowing what our finish line looks like is critical for the successful use of our benchmarks. If we do not know where we are going, or how many miles it is from where we are to that finish line, benchmarks don't work. As we check off each percentage point gained, pound lost, or dollar earned toward our goal, the finish line becomes less of a mental possibility and more of a absolute probability! "SO WHAT" is our odometer, our measuring stick.

4. *Now What?* Parking my bike, removing my helmet, and grabbing a few swallows of cool water, the event I enjoyed least and the ONE hurdle standing between me, the finish line, and my celebratory pasta with cream sauce loomed ahead. My preparations

for the 3-mile run had been an rigorous exercise in mind over matter. Summer vacations spent at Fallen Leaf had helped make me feel comfortable in lake water, and the wind in my face had made bike riding a joy over the previous months of training. Very little about the joint-pounding torture of running appealed to me. Rather than a runner's high, I frequently experienced pain, dizziness, and downright boredom.

Like the famous Little Engine that Could, I chanted "I think I can, I think I can" as I downed a quick swallow of water before setting out on the last portion of the race. This time, singing mental i-Tunes didn't help the run go by faster. Instead I found myself spotting a tree, or park bench, or person on the path ahead of me and counted the number of strides it took me to arrive at that future point on the trail. I tried not to think about my aching feet and concentrated instead on each step completed. I stopped twice for nasty cramps in my calf muscles. The run taunted me, stride by stride. Minutes dragged slowly on and my only solace came in the familiarity of the route around Lake Wilderness. When the course shifted back toward the park and the finish line, a quiet resolve set in and my stride took on new purpose and strength.

A volunteer seated in a folding lawn chair called out to me "You're almost there…keep running!" In the distance, I heard peppy music playing and microphone announcements as more competitors crossed the finish line. My lungs burned and strained to take in much-needed oxygen, yet my feet kept falling—one in front of the other.

At last, the finish line came into view and my head swirled with adrenaline as I saw and heard supportive cheers. Crossing the finish line, I clearly heard my mother's proud voice: "You can accomplish anything you set your mind to." Emotion overtook every muscle and I collapsed in a heaving mantra "I did it! I did it! I did it!"

NOW WHAT? Later that day, after my indulgent pasta lunch, in a moment of quiet reflection, my heart celebrated. Accomplishing something I had truly not thought possible filled me with a tingling excitement and a reassuring point of personal power. My mother's words rang over and over in my mind, and settled deeply in my heart: "You can accomplish anything you set your mind to." Quiet, joyful, grateful tears filled my eyes.

NOW WHAT? Armed with new belief that anything is possible, I enjoyed an afternoon of dreaming and imagining my next adventures, goals, and finish lines.

The point of personal power lies in the present moment as we race through life. Remember the questions:

What?
Gut?
So What?
Now What?

Crossing the finish line!

Anticipation!!!

PLANNING
Paddle Boat

To accomplish great things we must not only act, but also dream;
not only plan, but also believe.
—Anatole France

In the weeks leading up to our family's departure for Fallen Leaf Lake, my sister and I engaged in the childhood equivalent to strategic planning meetings. The purpose of these meetings was to map out our plan for our upcoming vacation, identifying milestones, deadlines and goals. After all, we wanted to ensure that no time went wasted at Fallen Leaf Lake. We took these planning meetings very seriously, scribbling notes to document our efforts.

For several summers at Sherman Cabin, we enjoyed the use of a bright yellow paddle-boat. This sturdy two-seater came equipped with an abundant area behind the seats for storage, as well as a shade canopy and, of course two cup holders cleverly positioned near the stick that connected to the craft's rudder. The yellow paddle-boat gave my sister and me increased freedom and mobility on the lake, plus a whole new slate of potential adventures.

On days when the late morning water of Fallen Leaf Lake did not begin to churn with summer breezes flowing down from Desolation Wilderness, Diana and I would often venture out on the boat. We'd paddle in the familiar direction of Rock Haven, Fallen Leaf Lodge, and The Store, hugging the shoreline as we peddled. I loved peering over the sides of the boat through the crystal-clear water all the way down to the lake bottom. The water of Fallen Leaf Lake is so clean and clear that even 20 or 30 feet from shore, we could still clearly make out rocks and logs and fish. The farther from shore we traveled, the bluer the water became. The deep water took on a magical quality and shimmered with sparkles of diamond-white sand that swirled in the deep, royal blue of the lake.

Every once in a while, rather than travel in the familiar direction, we'd break with tradition and pedal along the shoreline toward the far end of Fallen Leaf (closer to Lake Tahoe). The shoreline in this direction seemed more rugged and rocky to me. The cabins and docks were less familiar. And even on the calmest days, the breeze along this side of the lake was gusty and rough, which made the trip back to our dock longer and required more pedaling.

During one of our pre-vacation strategic planning meetings in our early teenage years, Diana and I decided we would make family history by taking our paddle boat all the way to the opposite side of the lake, to the mouth of Alpine Creek. We estimated that this journey would take all afternoon and as we discussed our goal, we factored in the best time of day for the least amount of boat traffic, how much food we would need to pack, and what we would do once we reached our exciting destination.

Then there was the *Mom Factor*. We knew our mother would not be as excited about our adventure as we were, for it meant dealing with boat traffic and deeper water and being well out of her range to come to our rescue. So part of our strategic planning included drafting a proposal to Mom, addressing what we guessed would be her most pressing concerns. Before we left for the lake that year, we presented our proposal and contingency plans to Mom while she sat on the couch in our family room.

We showed her our route, indicating familiar locations where we could take a break if we became tired (although in reality, in a paddle boat, if you are tired just stop pedaling!) We detailed for her our endurance-building plan, which included shorter rides in the first days of our vacation. We showed her a list of food we would pack and how we would store it behind the seats of the boat. Finally, we proposed that to help alleviate her worries about our safety, we would position a chair on the porch at Sherman Cabin with binoculars so she could easily track our progress. It took some doing, but Mom eventually approved our plan.

A few weeks later, with our Fallen Leaf Lake vacation in full swing, the morning of our adventure finally dawned. Diana and I quickly slipped from planning mode into implementation mode. We made our sandwiches and packed our snacks, cookies, chips, and fruit. We filled our canteens with cold water and packed *Dr. Pepper* for extra energy. We set up Mom's chair and binoculars on the porch and we slathered ourselves with sunscreen. Feeling completely prepared, we set out to make family history.

Our ride in the paddle boat was somewhat anti-climactic. Diana and I argued over who should control the steering (a point we hadn't discussed in our strategic planning sessions) and we both got a little tense when a motor boat zipped by, causing our small craft to bounce and sway in its wake. But we pedaled and we rested and we felt bold and independent. We watched the color of the lake water change from crystal clear, to murky bluish - green and then to dark royal blue. We pedaled faster to catch up with a small family of ducks floating on the water. We pedaled slower when we were caught in a wind gust.

Eventually, finally, we arrived at the mouth of Alpine Creek, whose waters had journeyed from the highest mountains to blend with those of our beloved Fallen Leaf Lake. Frankly, there wasn't much to see at the mouth of the creek. I'm not sure what I was expecting, but the reality was pretty boring. The strong and rushing creek we played by and marveled at up by the falls just kind of petered out here at the mouth. The water of the creek became very shallow and what looked like a shelf of river rock and pebbles eventually dropped off into the deeper water of the lake.

Diana and I looked around and even pulled the boat up onto the rocky shelf and waded around in the ankle-deep water. We ate our lunch on the paddle boat and then shoved off back in the direction of our cabin. Mom was still sitting on the porch with the binoculars when we arrived back safely, feeling triumphant and also a little disappointed.

Pebble to Ponder

Planning is essential when reaching for our goals, our targets, and our dreams. Some people seem to have a natural knack for planning, while others find the task difficult and tedious. The act of true planning goes beyond visualizing and dream-mapping. Creating our reality on purpose rather than flying by the seat of our pants requires strategic intent.

The more thought and strategy we put into the *before*, the more smoothly the *during* goes. My sister and I discovered this more through instinct than education. Our strategic planning sessions included several critical details of our journey, as well as the resources we would require. Additionally, we attempted to anticipate the various obstacles we would face (including Mom's lack of approval) and how to solve them.

I believe in Stephen Covey's philosophy, "begin with the end in mind," when it comes to planning. Visualizing the goal, end result, or destination first and then stepping backwards through what it takes to reach our *end*. The practice of breaking the larger goal or target into smaller bites is a time-tested principle of goal-getting.

Being able to adapt and adjust when unanticipated details arise (like who is going to steer the paddle boat) comes when we make the shift from planning to implementation. Having a plan is the first step, executing the plan and adjusting when necessary is just as critical to the achievement of our goals.

Whether the final destination or achievement provides us with our anticipated reward or sense of accomplishment is irrelevant. We may find we have more or less control on the outcome of a situation based on a direct result of the planning we invested prior to the undertaking. It is nearly always enlightening to reflect *after* the destination is reached on the lessons learned from planning an implementation. We can always find tweaks and adjustments that will make the next adventure even more successful and exhilarating.

Mom and Sheri on Mount Cathedral

PRACTICAL
Wingmen

A friend is someone with whom you dare to be yourself.
—Frank Crane

I am a frequent flyer. I love to fly. I love the feel of the accelerating engine as we charge the runway for take-off. I thrill as we climb up above the clouds and reach our cruising altitude. I marvel at the unique perspective of landmarks and cities as I gaze out the window. I'll admit I don't pay close attention to the flight attendant's briefing of oxygen masks and seat belts any more. I am usually comfortably seated with my pillow and my book long before the pre-flight speech begins. A while back, on a flight from Minneapolis to Seattle, I heard something different that caused me to put my book down.

"Ladies and Gentleman, greetings from the flight deck. If you're wondering why we haven't pushed back from the gate, we're waiting for our wingmen to arrive. We can't leave without them." I glanced at my watch and then peered out the window to see if I could spot the mysterious wingmen.

After probably hundreds of flights, I learned on this flight that wingmen are the guys you see with the big orange sticks standing outside the plane whenever leaving or arriving at the gate. My first impression of their function: wave the orange sticks by the wings of the plane.

I gazed out the window and decided to pay closer attention to the apparently critical function the wingmen played in my departure. I saw two guys in bright orange vests with matching bright orange sticks running toward my plane. Each claiming a wing, they wasted no time and immediately began to work. Sitting there as a premier-level frequent flyer, usually preoccupied with itineraries, gate numbers and connection times—I realized I'd never noticed the wingmen before. I studied them, fascinated as they carefully guided our plane back from the gate.

Keeping an eye on everything else moving on the tarmac from other planes, luggage carts, catering and fuel trucks, our orange-vested guides made our departure safe. The wingmen could see what the pilot and Air-Traffic control couldn't—all the little movements happening close to our plane and every obstacle on the ground. Waving their orange sticks, they led us, and once we were clear, I noticed the wingman on my side of the plane salute the pilot with his orange stick and smile. Having completed their critical function for our plane, our dutiful wingmen hurried off to assist another eager customer.

Without the wingmen, we couldn't leave the gate.

Pebble to Ponder

Wingmen are practical, level-headed, and efficient. Without our wingmen handling our everyday matters, we cannot leave the gate.

Wingmen guide and direct our movements as we navigate tight and narrow paths. Not only do they guide us, they do so with level heads, common sense, and without being caught up in everyday drama and tragedy. From their perspective, they have a simple function: to guide us from the gate to the runway without having us crash into anything. A simple focus with profoundly important consequences

Personal or career coaches definitely qualify as wingmen. An effective coach asks clarifying questions and allows us to discover the answers. Coaches don't provide advice or therapy, but rather, like the wingmen, help identify obstacles so we can take off in the direction of our dreams and goals. Coaches don't set our goals, objectives, and destinations for us, but rather provide a sounding board to evaluate the strength of our goals and detail of our plan to achieve them.

Friends and colleagues also serve as excellent wingmen. They help us see the obstacles and dangers of the ground that we cannot see. In my full-time job, a small group of trusted colleagues and I enjoy a wingmen relationship. We each manage a different geographic region of the country and only see one another a handful of times a year for business strategy meetings and company sponsored events. When one of us has a burr stuck in our bonnet about a corporate decision, or a challenge we can't seem to find a solution for in our regions, we assemble in *Meeting Room No. 5*—our safe place where we assume the role of either the pilot or the wingman. In this setting, usually in a lounge with our favorite happy hour beverages, we freely and trustingly share with each other.

Those of us playing the wingmen first listen and observe, then wave our orange sticks and recommend a safe and obstacle free route away from the gate.

Trips to the mall to purchase new clothing is another common example of the influence my wingmen friends provide. I may shy away from a particular style or color of clothing, blinded by the obstacles of body image or stubbornly held beliefs of what I would NEVER wear. My trusted wingmen are able to see what I cannot see and convincingly wave their orange sticks until I agree to take a risk with something new.

Who are your wingmen? Do you pay attention when they wave their orange sticks? Do you allow them to lead you out of danger and toward the runway so you can take off?

If you feel stuck at the gate, connect with your wingmen and let the power of that relationship guide you safely on your journey! Being coach-able means we are open to feedback and guidance from our wingmen. We let go of our need to completely control the situation and allow the wingmen to recommend a safe path.

PROACTIVITY
Yellow-Headed Bird

A bird does not sing because it has an answer.
It sings because it has a song.
—Chinese proverb

Sprinkled throughout our family photo albums, in our recorded almanac of proof of the magical moments spent at Fallen Leaf Lake, are several interesting pictures my mother took of a yellow-headed bird. We'd be out for a stroll along the creek to the falls, or sitting on the sunny porch in the late afternoon, or snacking on a delicious mint chocolate chip ice cream cone near the store, when my mom's favorite bird would burst into view. On lucky days, Mom, at the ready with our family Instamatic camera, would snap a hasty shot. Equally as often we'd be delighted by the sudden appearance of this strikingly bright bird when the camera was tucked away in Mom's purse back at the cabin.

"Darn, where is my camera?!" Mom would exclaim in frustration when the bird caught us by surprise.

Mom's favorite bird, in fact, is the Western Tanager, said to be one of the most colorful birds of the Lake Tahoe basin. The adult male has a bright red face and yellow nape, shoulder, and rump, with black upper back, wings, and tail. These birds are often out of sight, foraging high in trees, sometimes flying out to catch insects in flight. They mainly eat insects, fruits and berries. The brightness of their striking yellow and red feathers against the blue sky above Fallen Leaf Lake and the bright green of the pines made them even more magnificent in contrast to their surroundings. While Mom didn't know these birding facts, she referred to the Western Tanager as her favorite bird and longed to capture proof of its amazing beauty on film to show our friends back home.

Some years, the bird seemed to follow Mom around and would appear with regularity, begging for a close-up portrait. On those family vacations when the bird chirped and followed and posed, Mom kept the camera close and at the ready. She didn't want to be caught without her film and made an attempt to capture the tanager whenever he appeared. Other years, we'd go the full two weeks without seeing the brilliant yellow creature at all, and Mom would make a pouty, sad face and say, "Where is my yellow-headed bird?"

Shot after shot, year after year, Mom continued on her quest for photos of her favorite bird.

Those were the days when only Polaroid® cameras provided instant pictures. Our family Kodak Instamatic 104® camera didn't even have a zoom function and was basically point-and-shoot. Pictures needing flashes required a flash cube that snapped into the top of the camera and gave the photographer four opportunities for an extra flash of light before needing replacement. And of course, the film had to be transformed into pictures by the photo lab at the drug store. Because of these technical limitations,

Mom wasn't able to see the yellow-headed bird shots until well after our family vacations ended. Each year with anticipation, Mom would sift through the envelopes of captured memories, believing this would be the year the bird would smile back at her from a photograph. And every year, littered in the piles of pictures were shots of trees, shrubs, branches and sky, where Mom had seen the bird—but the elusive winged creature did not appear in the photographs.

Mom turned this trick of luck into a long-running family joke in our photo albums. Beneath a picture of a tree, shrub, branch or sky where the Western Tanager was supposed to be saying "Cheese," Mom would write "Where is the bird?", or "Can you see the bird?", or "Such a pretty bird!" to remind us of her photographic *faux pas*.

As the years rolled by and technology advanced, our instamatic camera was eventually replaced with one with a zoom function and lots of bells and whistles. Still the yellow-headed bird eluded Mom's lens and never found a place in our family photo almanac.

Pebble to Ponder

Mom experienced more opportunities to take shots of the Western Tanager when she acted proactively. With her camera close and flash loaded, little time was wasted when the bird appeared for her to get ready to take its picture. I remember Mom sitting on the small porch of *Eagle's Eyrie*, a small studio cabin rented each summer by our dear friends, Rod and Jesse Boyer.

Eagle's Eyrie sat high on a hillside and looked out over the tree tops. Here was prime opportunity for glimpsing the Western Tanager. Mom would spend the afternoon talking with Jesse on the porch, her crochet project on her lap and the camera next to her on the arm of the chair. When her bird would choose to appear, Mom would seamlessly disengage from her crochet hook and yarn, whisper "Oooh, there you are…" and raise the camera to click the picture.

Contrast this with the more reactive approach to capturing the bird on film. Without the camera nearby when we were out on a hike or down by the marina and store, there was little we could do when the Western Tanager appeared. "Darn, where is my camera?!" and a missed opportunity. Reacting from Sherman Cabin when the bird appeared was easier, yet always yielded disappointing results as well. The bird would appear perched on a branch and Mom would call to me: "Sheri, tippy-toe into my bedroom and bring me the camera… Hurry, my bird is here." I dutifully obeyed, yet without fail, the bird would either fly off before I returned with the camera, or be frightened off by the sounds of prepping the camera once I fetched it.

We are often happier with the results of proactive activity versus reactive activity. Anticipation and preparation send the message that we are ready for opportunity and opportunity is usually what shows up. Just like musicians can often predict the next phrase of notes in a score, we are more able to recognize and respond when opportunity appears.

Waiting to react, being caught off guard or unprepared, is an unsettling and frustrating feeling. We can sometimes salvage opportunity when responding reactively, but more often than not, we either don't recognize the chance when it arrives or spend valuable time in ad hoc preparation that ends in a disappearing opportunity.

I'm not suggesting that we are able to accurately predict when Western Tanagers will appear in our everyday routines of family, personal relationships, and career. Just as sometimes the bird appears without warning, we too are often surprised by the arrival of an opportunity or challenge. Reacting to sudden changes or challenges is clearly part of our living and growing journey. We can, however, identify tools and trends to aid us in being ready—being proactive. Tools, like the camera, film, and flash bulbs aided Mom in feeling confident she would have what was needed to immortalize the bird in our family album. Additionally, spending long afternoons on the porch at Eagles Eyrie, or at Sherman Cabin helped Mom identify the bird's behavior trends so she could better predict what time of day, and from which direction the Tanager would appear.

Finding ways to proactively approach the opportunities life affords us can help us walk more confidently, feeling prepared for what shows up tomorrow. I keep my camera on and in stand-by mode whenever I return to Fallen Leaf Lake. I am still searching for just the right moment to snap a portrait of Mom's Western Tanager.

Anything is possible—just don't look down!

POSSIBILITY
Climbing a Tree

If we did all the things we are capable of doing,
we would truly astound ourselves.
—Thomas Edison

I woke up one morning four years ago and recognized I LOVED my job! On my frequent business trips, I stayed in hotels with plush linens and concierge folk to make restaurant suggestions. On lucky occasions, I received upgrades to first class on my flights. My wardrobe had been upgraded to colorful, whimsical clothing rather than dull, corporate power suits. In my work, I felt challenged, effective and competent. Then came the call from the boss sharing that five of my colleagues and I would be attending a leadership seminar.

The fall air on the California coast was cool and misty; marine layer clouds covered the rolling hills. My colleagues and I were instructed to report at 7:00 a.m. in comfortable, layered clothing and sturdy walking shoes. Still sipping English Breakfast tea, I boarded a bus with 50 strangers and my five colleagues, unsure what this leadership seminar would include. A long and winding bus ride through the coastal hills eventually dumped us at our classroom for the day—a ropes course!

We tromped along the damp wooded path that wound up and alongside a narrow creek to a clearing. My heart began to beat harder as I gazed at the scene before me. A 30-foot ladder was lashed to a tree that had been stripped of branches and rigged with what looked like giant staples placed strategically on the sides of the tree. I let my eyes travel up the trunk of the tree—the top must have been 100 feet higher than where I stood on the forest floor.

We were instructed that our task would be to each take turns climbing the tree. The goal of the leadership exercise: climb to the top of the tree, jump off to catch a trapeze and swing through the tree tops like Tarzan. I remember thinking—"NO WAY—they can't make me do this—this is NOT in my job description!" I remember feeling out of control, doubtful that I had the skill to perform this task and frightened from head to toe.

The next thing I knew, I had been equipped with a crash helmet and harness. The harness, rigged with clips and ropes, would provide for my safety as I climbed. There was no escape. The forest and strangers around me took on a surreal quality, almost as if I had become a character in a Saturday morning cartoon. Standing at the base of the ladder, with sweaty palms and my heart thumping, there was nothing left to do but climb.

I should mention that our instructions were to climb as high as we felt we could. As I peered up the ladder, I determined before starting my accent that I would feel successful when I climbed to the top of the 30-foot ladder. I had no intention of continuing up the tree. So I began my climb. One carefully placed step at a time. Step. Step.

Step. My arms reached for the next higher rung on the ladder. Step. Step. The noise from those on the ground became more faint. Step. I fell into a rhythm consistent with the thumping of my heart. Step. Step. One more step. I had climbed to the top rung of the ladder.

I remember feeling surprisingly exhilarated. Climbing perhaps wasn't as difficult as I had first thought, as long as I took one step at a time. In that instant, I found courage welling up and determined to continue up the tree. Ladder rungs were replaced by the carefully spaced giant staples, which served to slow my climb as I became more aware of each foot and hand placement. Step. Pause. Step. Pause. Look up. Step. Pause. Step. The voices from the ground faded completely away so that the only sounds I heard were the birds and the breeze singing through the branches of the trees surrounding me.

Higher and higher I stepped…until…I reached the last staple on the tree. I did not feel exhilarated in this instant, however, as I considered my position for the first time. There were no more staples to grab, and in order to continue my task, I needed to be standing on TOP of the tree, not clinging to the side of it (my current position.) A new wave of fear and panic spread over me as I pondered how to adjust my position.

From the ground I heard voices chanting. The realization of what they were saying came to me like tuning into the clock radio as it clicks on in the morning, waking me from sleep. From the distant ground below, the words began to arrive: "LET GO. STEP UP. LET GO. STEP UP. STAND UP." Certainly the elevation was playing tricks on my brain—"LET GO? Are they CRAZY? I'm 100 feet off the ground! I will fall! I cannot let go of the tree!"

"LET GO. STEP UP. LET GO."

Perhaps it was fatigue. Perhaps it was the cramping of the muscles in my legs. Perhaps it was feeling my sweaty hands losing their grip on the staples. Or perhaps it was remembering that I had been hooked into a harness with pulleys and ropes rigged through the trees. The ropes were steadied by a group of three strong men on the ground. Perhaps I could just let go and step up. So, finding a droplet of courage and fighting with my fears, I released my hold on the staples and took one more step.

Adrenaline is a strange sensation. In this instant, adrenaline made my whole body shake. I found my hands, arms, legs and even my teeth trembling as I stood, carefully balanced on the top of this tree in the middle of the forest. In like fashion, the tree began to sway back and forth in sync with my shaking body. I don't know what made me think that a tree would be stationary and still, but the swaying did not serve to calm my already frazzled nerves. The tree began to creak as it swayed. CREAK. SWAY. CREAK.

From the ground, the chorus rose again. This time, the voices said: "THE TREE IS NOT SHAKING—YOU ARE." These people were obviously not experiencing the same thing I was. I am clearly NOT the cause of this sound… CREAK. The chorus chimed: "TAKE A DEEP BREATH." Rationally, this suggestion made sense to me. I raised my arms level with my shoulders and inhaled. I closed my eyes and slowly exhaled. When all the air had been expelled, I opened my eyes. All around me, the tree tops stood in support. My tree had stopped swaying. The sun in an instant broke through the coastal clouds and dancing sunbeams surrounded me. I felt completely free.

Only one final task remained. I was still 100 feet off the ground. Climbing back down the way I had clambered up didn't seem at all appealing. Suspended in front of me, about 10 feet from where I stood on top of my tree, a trapeze hung, beckoning me. Unfortunately, the beckoning trapeze meant leaving the safety and freedom of my triumphant perch atop the tree. My heart began to thump again. And from the ground, the annoying chorus began again to chant.

"JUMP! JUMP! JUMP!"

"No way! I can't jump that far."

"JUMP!"

"I can't!"

"ONE MORE STEP!"

One more filling inhale, then… I remember pushing off with my feet. I remember reaching upward, forward with every inch of my arms and fingertips. I remember closing my fingers in a grip. I remember just missing and not catching the trapeze.

I did not fall. The ropes held me firmly and securely 100 feet above the ground. The men below slowly began to carefully, tenderly, lower me back to the forest floor. Gratitude and contentment filled me as I glided downward. As I let go of the sky and the tree tops, I began to crave the company of the waiting chorus below. DOWN. Down. Down. Back to the strangers. Back to my colleagues. Back to the waiting chorus. Back to the rustic classroom in the woods that taught me more about leadership than any book I've read.

Pebble to Ponder

The day spent climbing the tree taught me about possibilities. These lasting reminders about what is POSSIBLE serve as guideposts as we work toward any goal, dream or corporate objective.

Take just one more step. How often do we limit what WE think is possible in our lives? We are comfortable, or think we can go no further. Why rock the boat? Why take that risk? Taking ONE more step, or taking action—even a small one gives us the gift of motivation to take another. As we step and celebrate each mini-win, we begin to embrace the POSSIBLE.

Let go and trust the ropes. Sometimes the only way to stand up is to let go! The safety of holding tightly to our trees can prevent us from achieving our final goal. We are all held up by ropes and if we are willing to trust them, we can find ourselves stepping up to a new level of what is POSSIBLE.

The tree is not shaking, YOU are. In the midst of a climb, we can become distracted by the energy and adrenaline of the experience. Our tree will sway and shake and feed our feelings of insecurity and fear. By taking time to center ourselves, pause, take deep filling breaths, we can find calm and resolve. We find the peace of the sun breaking though the coastal clouds. We find clarity and reconnect with what is POSSIBLE.

Leap! After all the preparation and climbing, trusting and centering, we each reach a point in our striving where we have a choice to make. Stay where we are or leap! Taking the leap is all about pushing off from the safety of what is familiar and trusting that the leap will lead to an even greater realization of the POSSIBLE.

The waiting chorus. On the ground looking up, stands the waiting chorus—the voices known and unknown shouting messages to support us in our climbing. The waiting chorus cheers for our success and is observant of our hesitations and triumphs. When our head is cloudy and distracted, the waiting chorus sings of what is POSSIBLE.

PREPARATION
Batteries and Tow Trucks

You have brains in your head,
You have feet in your shoes,
You can steer yourself,
Any direction you choose.
—Dr. Seuss

For a family of four, we packed HEAVY for our annual sojourns to Fallen Leaf Lake. In addition to the varied clothing needed for a two-week vacation without laundry facilities, we'd carry sleeping bags, bath linens, and enough food to easily last a month. Add to this our entertainment items to amuse us for our annual retreat—games, puzzles, and various necessities for playing at the lake—water toys, flippers/masks/snorkels, heavy-duty inner tubes, and our paddle boat. We could easily fill more than one vehicle with our packing, leaving little to no room for the human cargo.

While I'm not absolutely certain the rationale was more complicated than readying our enormous pile of packed provisions, one summer as we prepared to head to our cabin, we filled TWO vehicles to the brim.

On the morning of our departure, Dad and Diana climbed into one car and Mom and I set out in the second vehicle, determined to keep pace with Dad as he sped along the Interstate toward Fallen Leaf Lake. These were the wondrous years before cell phones and pagers, so we kept tabs on each other by pre-arranging meeting spots along the familiar journey—the first being the Nut Tree Resort, a mere 60 miles from our driveway in Concord.

Mom and I were first to arrive at the Nut Tree, but only moments before Dad's truck pulled up next to us. We stretched and Diana and I shared stories from the road—had she seen the Navy ships in Benicia, had she smelled the onions growing in the fields as we passed—touchstone topics that we checked off like completing a grocery list. As all seemed in order, we quickly re-joined the cars on the busy interstate, setting our next meeting place before we departed—Placerville. I waved good-bye to Diana as Dad sped past us on the freeway, neither of us imagining the adventure the rest of that day would bring.

Not long after my wave to Diana, our car began to make some very strange noises, and Mom began to worry. The engine coughed and surged—and unable to maintain freeway speeds, we were forced to pull off and find a gas station with men who knew more about what made cars work than either Mom or I.

My memory is a little fuzzy on the details of what exactly happened next. I DO remember stopping at a gas station where the car completely stalled and it was clear we wouldn't be traveling anywhere on our own. I DO remember Mom retrieving the dealership information out of the glove box and calling the dealer back in Concord of whom my father was a loyal customer. Then, I remember waiting. Waiting and wondering whether Diana and Dad had arrived in Placerville. Waiting and waiting. I remember Mom having another phone conversation with the car dealership—and then, not long after that, I remember a tow truck pulling up in front of our car with half of our Fallen Leaf supplies carefully packed inside and hooking us up to carry Mom and me all the way back to Concord.

Without any method to contact Dad and Diana, Mom and I were left to the mercy of mechanics and the belief that Dad would furiously wait in Placerville for only so long before continuing with Diana up the mountain highway leading to Fallen Leaf. As Mom and I traveled back to Concord with the tow truck driver, we imagined Dad and Diana arriving at the cabin and having everything unpacked before we joined them. I tried to push the worry away that kept fluttering around my face like a gnat—"How WILL we make it to the cabin without a car?"

Meanwhile, on the shores of Fallen Leaf Lake, Dad and Diana had arrived at the cabin without us. When Mom and I hadn't shown up in Placerville, Dad, true to his habits, huffed about Mom misunderstanding the meeting place and decided to make the rest of the drive without stopping. Diana's constant fretting finally led Dad to agree to check in at the Lodge office once arriving at Fallen Leaf for any messages from Mom and me. Once Dad and Diana had unpacked their portion of our hoard of supplies, they walked to the lodge to investigate our absence.

Back in Concord, the news of our ailing car was not good. I peered out the waiting room window at our vacation treasures hoisted 10 feet in the air while men in gray jumpsuits explored the underside and engine of our car. After more unbearable waiting, one of the men in gray approached my Mom to explain that the car needed more repair than could be done in a day and we would need to either wait until the next day to travel to Tahoe or use one of the dealer's loaner vehicles to make the trip. We opted for the latter and with the help of the mechanics, had soon transferred all our vacation gear to the unfamiliar car. Before leaving to re-start the road trip, Mom left a message at Fallen Leaf Lodge: "To John Hughey: Car broke down in Sacramento. Towed back to Concord. Leaving now in loaner car."

Back to the Interstate, past the Navy fleet in Benicia, the smell of the onions growing in the fields, and the Nut Tree Resort, Mom and I hummed along, feeling happy to be safely moving toward the blue Lake Tahoe waters and the rest of our family. The remainder of our journey passed without incident and we expected to arrive at the cabin to see Dad and Diana enjoying the view and the sunshine. The cabin, however, was empty—although our suitcases and sleeping bags lay strewn on the furniture and the refrigerator and cupboards held our vacation food. Dad, Diana, and the OTHER vehicle were missing! Thinking quickly, we left a note on the door saying we'd tromped off to the Lodge to search for them and began walking toward the hope of reunion at the Lodge.

As we approached the Lodge, I spotted Diana playing on the beach and ran toward her calling out—"We made it! We made it!" Diana instantly burst into tears as her guardian, a long-time family friend who spent every summer at Fallen Leaf Lake, joined us to explain Diana's outburst. "John received your message and left for Concord right away," offered Jesse.

Mom and I obviously looked confused as Jesse continued. "Your note said that the car had broken down and that you were stuck in Concord after being towed back to the dealership—John's on his way to pick you up—HOW did you get here?"

I'll skip many of the details from the rest of the story. After arriving back in Concord to discover we had been given a loaner car, Dad, for the third time in the same day, drove on the interstate that connected our home town to our vacation paradise. He arrived at our cabin, stiff and tired long after Diana and I had surrendered to sleep in our orange and blue striped sleeping bags. That was the only year we drove two vehicles to Fallen Leaf Lake.

Cars are a reminder for me that sometimes we are just not in control. Without alternatives, Mom and I were at the mercy of the car and the mechanics on that summer day so many years ago. Without a method to contact Dad and Diana, we were left to our best judgment on how reach our destination. I've never been very good not being in control. I can still remember feeling so irritated and uncomfortable with all the waiting and uncertainty that accompanied the Fallen Leaf breakdown of 1979. As an adult, I'm still given lessons in being prepared and the skill of letting go by my car.

Take for example, car batteries. A while back, on my way to Seattle for a meeting, I stopped off at the local UPS Store to send a couple of packages. I wasn't in the store for more than 20 minutes. When I got back to the car and attempted to start it… ZIPPO. No engine starting sounds. Terrific! My first thought was "I should have purchased some jumper cables at Target last week." (I hate those "shoulds.") Long story short, a nice young man from a nearby carwash gave my ailing battery a jump start, and off I sped down the road making it to my meeting in Seattle with time to spare.

A few days after the UPS store incident, I popped out to run some errands during lunch. Hopped in the car and set off with my list of four errands tucked in the visor. After making my last stop and popping back into the car to head home, guess what? Yep, ZIPPO sounds from the engine. Now I was REALLY mad with myself because, did I go purchase jumper cables after the last time this happened like I knew I should have? Nope. And there I was stuck again.

Pebble to Ponder

Batteries and tow trucks are metaphors for being prepared. Batteries make us go. Without a full charge, they weaken. If they get too weak, they simply fizzle out completely and need to be jump started so they can re-charge themselves. Another observation about batteries—after the jump start, running the engine for a while is necessary to strengthen the battery before turning the car off again…or…ZIPPO the next time you attempt to start the engine.

Batteries tested regularly help us avoid the chance of getting stuck without any power. Have you tested your Life Battery lately? Does it have a full charge? Or is it weakening? Do you need a jump start? What can you do today to strengthen that battery? And finally, if you've had a jump start recently, what are you doing to run your engine so that battery re-charges fully?

Jumper cables are handy tools to keep close at hand. People, favorite hobbies, and locations can all serve as life's jumper cables. Fallen Leaf Lake is still a jumper cable for me when I find myself low on battery reserves. Keep your jumper cables handy for when you need that extra JOLT!

Tow trucks are strong and can pull us when we have no power to go on our own. Tow trucks come to where we are—no matter where that might be from our driveway to a mountain pass to a gas station in Sacramento. And, when we completely break down, it's comforting to know that tow trucks can take us back to the mechanics bay to be hoisted, diagnosed, and repaired.

Dad always told me to check the oil and battery before embarking on any long road trip. Being PREPARED is always wiser than having to pay for costly towing and mechanic repairs. Regular maintenance is always more cost effective than emergency fixes. Keeping our batteries charged and jumper cables close at hand is good advice for life, too.

PLEASURE
Lemonade

Laughter is sunshine in any life.
—William Thackery

Life must be lived as play.
—Plato

One of the great joys of our Fallen Leaf Lake paradise was exploring the abundant back country of Desolation Wilderness. While we didn't join the heavy-hitting backpackers who would set off for a multi-night communion with nature, we enjoyed day hikes to alpine lakes, hidden springs, and waterfalls far away from the sound of motor boats and tourists. Nearly every year, we'd choose from our favorite destinations and spend a few days in advance of the hike reviewing maps, planning our menu of snacks, and re-adjusting to the cramped feeling of double socks inside our hiking boots.

On our list of top five hikes: Angora Lakes. Nestled above Fallen Leaf Lake, this twin lake destination offered a unique combination of a challenging hike toward Angora Peak, and a small summer resort complete with a deli/store, a coarse white sand beach, and free entertainment! OK, I should probably clarify a few of the details here. In truth, Angora Lakes boasted private cabins and homes accessible via a steep and narrow dirt road that wound up through a series of blind switchback turns, from a difficult-to-find, unmarked turn off from Fallen Leaf Road. The road eventually ended at a parking area connected to a mostly flat gravel trail leading to Angora Lakes.

Although I'm not absolutely certain, I always assumed that the folks who owned the cabins up at Angora had to pack in their supplies as the trail wasn't wide enough to accommodate vehicles. The real hike to Angora Lakes, however, emerged from a small trail head just near the campsites by Alpine Creek at Fallen Leaf Lake. We loved this hike because it was possible to meet up with Mom and Dad and provisions from the car and enjoy a picnic lunch and swim in addition to the hike—a wonderfully perfect combination of exercise, accomplishment, and relaxing recreation!

The free entertainment at Angora Lakes came from the crazy teenagers who climbed a cliff that seemed 100 feet above the lake to jump into the water below. The coarse white sandy beach included bits of pine bark and needles, and lots of big black ants, so we were always grateful for the towels that magically arrived from the car in the parking lot. And finally, the deli. I honestly don't remember ever ordering anything to eat there. What I do remember, very clearly, was packing loose change in my pockets to purchase a plastic cup of the most amazingly sweet and delicious lemonade my young taste buds had ever experienced! Better than the picnic or the cooling swim in the shallow lake, or watching the "crazy teenagers" leap from the cliff—that lemonade was THE reason to hike to Angora Lakes.

This lemonade did not come from crystallized powder or a frozen concentrate can. The lemonade at Angora was the real, homemade kind from fresh lemons, squeezed by hand, sweetened with sugar (the real stuff), and served in a tall plastic cup with ice and a lemon wedge for presentation. Ahhhh. The thirst-quenching mixture always tasted perfect. As I tried to make it last, each slow swallow would tingle my tongue and cool my throat. I remember dreaming about owning a home at Angora Lakes and having a glass of this bright yellow elixir every single day! Yes, I'd live up here, at Angora Lakes, drink lemonade everyday, and raise "crazy teenagers" who would jump into the lake and provide the hikers with free entertainment. However, I'd have to do something about these annoying black ants on the beach. I couldn't have been more content with those sweet sips of pleasure and day dreams if a stranger had walked up to me and placed a million dollars in my lap.

These delicious moments of pure pleasure on a sunny summer day, drinking lemonade and dreaming of a carefree life would stay with me after the picnic ended and the afternoon shadows lengthened. Tingling, day-dreamy pleasure after draining every last drop of lemonade, after lacing up the hiking boots again, and all the way back down the winding narrow hiking trail. Sweet lemony tastes on my lips all the way back to the campground at Fallen Leaf Lake. Back down the road toward Sherman Cabin. Smiling and dreaming sweet satisfying dreams with each step.

Pebble to Ponder

Somewhere along the journey from childhood to adulthood, we forget to notice brilliant lemonade. Moments of sweet day-dreamy pleasure are fewer and farther between. We plan vacations and "stay-cations" and then set about filling them to the brim with tours, excursions, and sights to see. Rarely do we sit quietly, letting coarse, warm, white sand squish between our toes or take time to slowly sip each miraculous taste of perfect lemonade.

We over-schedule, over-commit, over-extend and over-work ourselves and lemonade (sweetened artificially) rarely accompanies our mealtimes. Sweet pleasure, absent of obligation or expectation is pushed aside for more important tasks. While we may lead lives filled with efficiency and success, we lose the tingly pleasure of real, hand-squeezed, perfect lemonade.

The good news—the ingredients needed to reclaim our lemony pleasure exist abundantly all around us. Spend time picking the lemons by choosing the activity, destination or feeling that will bring you the sweetest satisfaction. Squeeze out the juice by hand and clear the cluttering distractions and obligations that can block your efforts. Sweeten the moment by sharing your lemonade moments with someone who makes your life more complete. Then, simply sit on a white, sandy beach and savor each simple, perfect, pleasurable taste. Ahhhhhhhhhhh.

PRIDE
Rock Haven

*There are only two ways to live your life. One is as though
nothing is a miracle. The other is as though
everything is a miracle.*
—Albert Einstein

Nearly halfway between Sherman Cabin and the store and marina at Fallen Leaf Lodge sits a castle made of rocks. The estate known as Rock Haven captured my imagination in ways no other home at Fallen Leaf did. Like many of the residences at Fallen Leaf, Rock Haven's property extended to both sides of the road. The main structure sat away from the road with a semi-circle driveway flanked on either side by rock columns bearing brass plaques with the proud words: "Rock Haven, 1932 Wm. Maderious."

Behind the main house, even further up the hillside, stood great outdoor fire pits with chimneys and several cottages. On the lake side, a vast terrace of rock steps, more areas for picnics and bonfires stretched from the edge of the road all the way to the water. The mysterious property was crowned with a large, green boathouse whose walls were painted the same shade of green as the other buildings of the estate.

We knew very little about the history of Rock Haven beyond the stories we heard from our Fallen Leaf connections and conversations over dinner or while floating on an inner tube in our lake. The version of the truth I remember goes something like this: William Maderious was a wealthy industrialist from the San Francisco area who built Rock Haven for his wife and gave it to her as a wedding present in 1932.

Rock Haven stood as a proud constant along the road to the store and Fallen Leaf Lodge. Armed with the story I had been told about the mansion's origins, I imagined Rock Haven to be a place where the rich and famous would gather and have grand summer parties with hundreds of guests. When feeling especially sneaky and brave, Diana and I would duck under the heavy black chain that hung between short fencelike columns and explore the lakeside terrace. I'd close my eyes and imagine ladies in soft pastel dresses, carrying parasols and drinking tea from delicate porcelain cups as they looked out over the blue water of Fallen Leaf Lake.

As Diana and I would climb around on the rocky structure, we'd envision boats leaving the boathouse and dock for a short cruise along the lakeshore. We could almost smell the chicken and pork rib barbeque. We could almost taste the lemonade and potato salad and homemade ice cream as we created story after story of the visitors to Rock Haven.

Our visions of parties and grand people at Rock Haven lived vibrantly in our minds. In reality, Rock Haven was nearly always boarded up, standing locked and lonely summer after summer. We'd study the buildings and grounds for signs that someone had visited to enjoy the view or at least taken the boat for a spin. Mystery surrounded Rock Haven and even when it was evident that the estate was empty and completely void of inhabitants, Diana and I felt profoundly guilty of our trespassing adventures on the lakeside terrace.

From our own dock at Sherman Cabin, Rock Haven's green boathouse was an easy-to-spot landmark, so it was nearly impossible to not think about the mysterious owners or what fine furnishings existed inside the mansion. I borrowed from the grandness of Rock Haven, from its perception of wealth, prosperity, and pride on many occasions. There was something magical about the mystery of this home, of its reason for being, that strengthened me like the rocks that so beautifully adorned the structures.

Pebble to Ponder

Just this year, on a return visit to Fallen Leaf Lake, some of the mystery surrounding Rock Haven vanished for me. As I made my way along the familiar road to the bend that opens up onto Rock Haven, I noticed the chains in the driveway removed, the windows open, and a jeep in the driveway! Drawing from the bravery of my youth and my trespassing imaginings, I walked right up to a man and his two dogs shoveling last remnants of the spring snow away from the garage, and introduced myself. The next thing I knew I was being led up the stairs and into the main structure at Rock Haven—the castle of my childhood memories.

Inside I found a small, humbly appointed home. A living room with a large fireplace stood in the center of the cabin. To the left were the bedrooms, and to the right of the family room were the newly remodeled kitchen and small dining area. The new owners had just arrived for the summer and were busily unpacking so I didn't linger. I discovered Rock Haven's new owners had purchased the estate from Mrs. William Maderious and were preparing the cabin for the arrival of their own children and grandchildren.

Though far from the castle I imagined, as I left Rock Haven, the same feelings of pride and love lingered in my mind. Obviously the terraced lakefront structure never hosted a summer party for hundreds of the rich and famous. Dozens of classic "Great Gatsby" cars probably never lined the side of the road, and perhaps Mr. and Mrs. Maderious didn't have a household staff living in the basement of Rock Haven after all. And maybe the boat house only ever sheltered a simple fishing boat and not a few well-appointed, grand yachts. Still, everywhere I looked at this aged cabin property, love and pride reigned.

Pride has many definitions and contexts. A sense of one's own worth or dignity, and something cherished, valued, or enjoyed well define the feelings of pride I experienced at Rock Haven. Walking along the property perimeter this spring, I thought more about Mr. Maderious as I imagined him creating this beautiful home out of love for his wife and family. Perhaps Mrs. Maderious really did enjoy a cup of tea from a delicate porcelain cup and Mr. Maderious wanted to create a terraced landscape in a perfect setting above the lapping water of the lake for his wife to take in the magnificent view.

As I studied the rocks that made up the fence posts, broad steps, and structures of Rock Haven, I imagined Mr. Maderious pushing a wheelbarrow filled with the stones he had collected along the hillside to create this haven. I bet he saved his favorite stones for the large fireplace centerpiece inside the cabin. I smiled as I thought of Mr. Maderious mounting the engraved metal markers that proudly announced his gift of love to the world: "Rock Haven: 1932 Wm. Maderious."

Where and who are the "something cherished, valued and enjoyed" for you? William Maderious created a tangible manifestation of the pride he felt for his wife and family. How do we manifest the pride we feel for those we cherish? How do we build a castle for them from hand selected stones? When we build up those around us by referring to them as "our pride and joy" or "our top salesman" or "our most profitable team," we are adding to the stones that build our rock havens. When we back those words up with the mortar of supportive action, our castles rise from the ground and becomes strong and impenetrable.

Building family, team, and corporate pride in this fashion contributes to unity of purpose, which in turn inspires contribution and ownership. We want to lend our efforts, expertise, and energy to making our rock haven even more spectacular, more cherished, more treasured. The synergy created when a collection of minds and hearts combines efforts is nothing less than a masterpiece.

Some may say that pride or feeling proud is something we should avoid, a sin, a weakness. Sometimes, however, we can see positive symbols of pride, in something cherished, valued, or enjoyed—like Rock Haven. Built from love, in a spirit of creating a legacy of beauty, a haven from the world, William Maderious' mysterious cabin in the woods at Fallen Leaf Lake is a symbol of strength, of worth, of dignity. If the stones at Rock Haven could talk, I imagine they'd say such pursuits are worthy of our journey.

The old road to Fallen Leaf Lake

PRIORITIES
Rules of the Road

Your success or failure in life will not be decided by the number
of setbacks you encounter, but rather how you react to them.
—Unknown

Navigating Fallen Leaf Road requires advanced driving skills. The short five-mile drive from Highway 89 to the Lodge is a winding, narrow, pot-hole-infested adventure. Fallen Leaf Road boasts no curbs or sidewalks or driveways—it is lined instead with large boulders, trees with roots that infringe on the asphalt, and creative wooden signs announcing the names and addresses of the cabins and homes.

As a young girl, I remember feeling a mixed anxiousness when we'd make the final turn from the highway to Fallen Leaf Road. Butterflies and excitement churned as I realized we were within minutes of our treasured destination. Diana and I would break into song: "Fallen Leaf, here we come. Right back where we started from..." (set to the tune

California, Here We Come). We'd strain our necks and peer out the windows, pointing out familiar sites as we crept along. This excitement mixed with apprehension as I hoped traffic would be light and the vehicles small.

Creeping along is about the best any driver can do on Fallen Leaf Road. Out at the highway, the road could almost pass as two lanes. Lucky drivers in vehicles smaller than full-sized RVs could usually pass oncoming cars with a foot or more distance to spare. Just beyond the old Forest Service Campground and fantastic wildflower and aspen meadow, however, the road quickly narrows and becomes barely wide enough for a sub-compact. My mother never drove this part of our journey and would sit in the front passenger seat with her eyes closed. "Oh, geeze, oh geeze…John, please be careful…oh geeze" became her constant mantra as we inched our way toward our final destination.

I never doubted my father's driving expertise. He had a system. He always managed to squeeze by the most narrow spots even when oncoming traffic was constant. Our hosts, the Cravens, called the weekends "in-and-out days," as most families would arrive or depart from their time at Fallen Leaf on Saturday or Sunday mornings. In-and-out days required that a few simple rules of the road be followed and I admired my father for being so calm and confident as he navigated. From my young eyes, the following were the rules of Fallen Leaf Road:

Rule #1: Roll down the driver's window and put your arm on the window ledge. This rule was non-negotiable and nearly EVERYONE followed it. In the years before automatic windows, I remember watching in amazement as drivers turning onto Fallen Leaf Road immediately began cranking their windows down. In the rare instance when a driver didn't comply with this rule, oncoming vehicles would signal by imitating the cranking gesture in the air between the cars. With the window down, drivers gained heightened perspective in judging the distance between vehicles. The arm on the window ledge served as an additional method for communicating with other drivers. Having complied with this rule, the brave drivers of Fallen Leaf Road were prepared to move forward.

Rule #2: Outbound cars have the right of way. When two cars met face to face on Fallen Leaf Road, one of them had to scoot off the road onto pullouts or driveways to let the other car squeeze by. Sometimes this scooting also required backing up by one or more cars. The Fallen Leaf equivalent of rush-hour traffic on weekend in-and-out days often included a backlog of several cars attempting to move far enough off the road to let the outbound traffic through.

Rule #3: Rule #2 is rescinded if outbound cars have a larger shoulder or if inbound cars will end up in the lake if they pull over. Sometimes it just wasn't possible for an inbound car to move far enough off the road to let the outbound car pass by. In some particularly tricky spots on Fallen Leaf Road, there is literally NO shoulder on the inbound side of the road, where there are steep vertical drops directly into the lake. These types of challenges were my father's specialty. He took great pleasure in scooting off the road when other drivers thought it impossible. My mother's chant of "oh geeze... OH GEEZE.... JOHN, PLEASE BE CAREFUL" escalated in volume and intensity in these tight moments. Dad would smile, crank the wheel while grunting a little, and miraculously 100% of the time, our vehicle remained on the road and did not end up in the lake.

Rule #4: Always smile and wave when passing another driver. Whether on the inbound our outbound side of the road, Rule #4 was essential. My father loved Rule #4.

Even in the 1970s and 1980s, road rage and impatience with fellow drivers reigned on the busy Northern California freeways we were accustomed to driving. Fallen Leaf Road invited all drivers and all vehicles to take a step backward in time to a season when neighbors smiled and greeted each other as they passed. In that briefest moment, inbound and outbound cars and cargo connected, the outbound driver feeling sad at having to leave Paradise, and the inbound driver brimming with anticipation. Both communicated understanding with the simplest gestures of a smile and a wave.

Pebble to Ponder

Few examples illustrate the battle of competing priorities better than driving on Fallen Leaf Road. In the traffic and static that clog up our lives, the simple rules for success on Fallen Leaf Road can also serve us as we meet an oncoming priority head on. With so much to accomplish on the road to our final destination, knowing how to successfully squeeze by, scoot out of the way and accurately judge the distance between our priorities is essential. Additionally, we all experience in-and-out days, when the number of our incoming and outgoing priorities becomes so heavy we can feel like nothing is able to squeeze through.

The difficult part of juggling priorities is knowing where to give prime attention when two or more tugs on our heart are equally important. Which is the larger vehicle— an opportunity to provide service for a neighbor family, or an outdoor adventure with your sixteen-year-old and his closest friends? Who gets the right of way—the extra project for the boss that will yield a monetary bonus, or re-staining the back deck on the last sunny weekend of the summer in preparation for the upcoming winter? How do you successfully navigate the potholes, RVs and boat trailers, and avoid ending up off the shoulder altogether?

The secret to success is in Rule #4: "Always smile and wave when passing another driver." Successfully juggling priorities and embracing balance absolutely requires connection with our fellow drivers. In making room for others and sharing the road, we find that both incoming and outgoing priorities are met. As we connect with each other, smiling and waving as we pass, we communicate understanding. In community, our priorities are no more or less important than that of our neighbor.

Whenever I return to Fallen Leaf Lake, I still follow the rules, crank my window down, and smile and wave at everyone I pass. The connection feels good, like the ultimate priority.

camping life—Dad and Sheri ca 1966

PORTION
Biscuits and Gravy

*Things that matter most must never be at the mercy of things
that matter least.*
—Goethe

At Fallen Leaf Lake, Dad was the cook. He had two essential rules in his camping kitchen: #1) always cook with butter, and #2) meat (preferably pork or beef) must be served with every meal. Not surprisingly, friends and family who visited us during our annual stays at Sherman Cabin understood that light cuisine and leafy greens would be scarce at mealtime. Attempts at portion control were also discouraged as leaving the table hungry or leaving uneaten food on your plate was the ultimate insult.

Breakfast was Dad's favorite meal to prepare, and a staple Fallen Leaf Lake breakfast was biscuits and gravy. This feast, saved for special occasions or visitors typically included Jimmy Dean Sausage patties, crispy fried bacon, Grands biscuits, scrambled eggs, sliced beef steak tomatoes, and Dad's signature milk gravy, flavored with the fat of bacon and sausage. Because this mouth-watering meal was so filling and difficult to push away, eating the biscuits and gravy breakfast usually meant skipping lunch and just snacking until dinner. After all, there is sometimes too much of a good thing!

I remember the most difficult and time consuming part of preparing biscuits and gravy was getting the gravy just right. Dad didn't follow a recipe, but knew how the gravy was supposed to look as he prepared the creamy concoction. Starting with his special gravy-making, cast-iron skillet, Dad would add sausage drippings and flour to the pan until the paste had the right color. Pouring in the milk meant constant stirring to work out all the lumps as the flour dissolved. Then came the waiting—waiting for the gravy to thicken as it heated. Stirring patiently, Dad would whistle as he watched for the milky bubbles to form. If everything went smoothly, the gravy would bubble at the moment the biscuits in the oven turned a light, warm brown.

Anticipation gave way to delight as the fluffy biscuits, topped with sausage, fresh sliced tomato and gravy satisfied our hungry mountain appetites. Scrambled eggs and bacon on the side (because protein is a good way to start the day) finished off the tasty temptations. While the food on our table was always abundant, leaving uneaten food on your plate was discouraged, so judging the portion became an important skill. I learned it was better to go back for several small helpings and gauge my hunger level as I went, rather than fill my plate to bursting at the beginning of the meal. I saved room for my favorite elements of the meal, the bacon for example, and would add extra slices to my plate as a reward for judging my portions well.

The cabin smelled of bacon, sausage and gravy for most of the day following a biscuits-and-gravy breakfast, a satisfying reminder of a savory beginning to what was sure to be another magnificent day at Fallen Leaf Lake.

Pebble to Ponder

How many times did my mother warn me: "Don't bite off more you than you can chew." She didn't like feeling overwhelmed, stretched thin, or stressed out, and took ample opportunity to warn her over-achieving daughter of the dangers of doing too much. "You can only do what you can do, Sheri."

Back in the 1970s and early 1980s, before cell phones, email, and text messaging, "biting off more than I could chew" meant over-committing to face-to-face activities—school obligations, church service projects, balancing homework, and a part-time job. With the additional time-eaters modern technology adds, I'm sure my mother would be shouting her warning from the rooftop!

We are all faced at some level with more to do than time, energy, or resources to do it. Competing demands and priorities throw our minds into chaos as we wrestle with imagined scenarios and plans to accomplish all of the important items on our "to do" lists. What it comes down to is time—how we use our daily allotment of 24 hours. How we dish up our portion of time, much like the biscuits-and-gravy breakfast at Fallen Leaf Lake, can either leave us feeling satisfied, or sick from over-indulgence.

Any student of nutrition or weight control knows, portion size is a key element to success in the battle of the bulge. We can eat ANYTHING (even biscuits and gravy) as long as we accurately and consistently serve up portion sizes that fit our specific needs.

Once we are done with the portion, another helpful weight control tip is to push the plate away, or put a napkin over your plate to signal to your brain that you are DONE. Many experts encourage eating on a small plate to trick your brain into thinking it's getting a FULL-sized meal because the plate appears more full.

Facing the savory temptation of a biscuits-and-gravy breakfast is much like facing our crazy concoction of life, and we can heed my mother's warning of not biting off more than we can chew by following the same principles used in nutrition.

Know your serving size and stick to it! We all know how much we can handle. We can recognize when we have too much to do—when our plate is too full. So rather than have to leave undone tasks on our plate, wouldn't it be wiser to dish up only what we know we can handle, and leave a little room for dessert (the sweet things in life that finish off any perfect meal)?

When we are done, let's push the plate away! Finishing our tasks shouldn't mean we feel compelled to take on more! Why not enjoy the satisfaction of completion, time to reflect and let the day settle, much like a scrumptious meal?

Use a smaller plate! Rather than getting fat on constantly trying to do more—be more places, work more hours, participate in more activities, why not focus on those things that truly satisfy us and partake of them on a smaller plate? Too many tasks on too big a plate ultimately mean we are unable to give our best to all of them. To feel more successful, more content, more satisfied, choosing which actions deserve our focus and room on our plate is vital.

PRINCIPLES
Don't Touch That!

Intellectuals solve problems; geniuses prevent them.
—Albert Einstein

A s a young "fallen-leafer" camping along Alpine Creek, I remember that our family relied on traditional camping equipment to make our roughing it vacation more comfortable. My earliest memories of Fallen Leaf are not of tent camping, but of a small camper that perched on the back of Dad's yellow pick-up truck. As a basic shell, it kept our sleeping quarters off the ground, housed our food in small cupboards, but provided few other creature comforts. We still used the common camp-ground outhouse—actually they were flushing toilets (a luxury), with one stall for women, and a stall for men on the opposite side. The line for women was always longer, no matter what time of day or night! We cooked on a camping stove, Dad chopped our firewood, and at night, we trusted flashlights and Coleman lanterns to provide light at our table.

Our green Coleman lantern fascinated me. It sat perched and dormant on our picnic table all day, with two white netted mantels hanging inside a clear glass dome. I didn't fully understand how, but when Dad fiddled with our Coleman each night, those little white mesh bags would produce bright white light once darkness fell. Watching Dad light our Coleman each night added to my curiosity about how the contraption worked.

First, Dad filled the container at the base of the lantern with kerosene through a small hole using a funnel. Then he unscrewed a hand pump on the other side of the base and began to pump air into the base of the lantern. Once finished with the pumping, Dad would secure the knob again and open our box of strike-anywhere wooden matches. He didn't light a match right away, but fiddled with the lantern some more, turning knobs and a hook-like lever near the base of the lantern. I sat with rapt attention as Dad, having completed the pre-lighting routine, struck a single match and held the small flame under the white net mantels. A second or two later, with a whoosh, the mantels would burst into bright, white light. It was the best magic trick I'd ever seen, and Dad performed it flawlessly every single night! Adjusting the knobs for optimal light, Dad would place the illuminated lantern on the center of our wood table where it would burn until we all turned in for the night.

Within moments of lighting our Coleman, and with the consistency of the cricket song surrounding us each night at dusk, my mother would emerge from the camper and utter a stern, three-word warning while pointing at the Coleman: "Don't touch that!" The soft hiss of the Coleman accompanied our evenings along Alpine Creek and gave bright light to the table where the grown-ups played *Aggravation* and laughed well into the summer night. Evening after evening, I would sit on the hard, wooden picnic bench and peer up at the magical light, listening to its hum and heeding my mother's warning: "Don't touch that!"

One evening, when I was about five years old, I found myself face to face with the Coleman lantern without parental supervision. Mom was dealing with my two-year old sister, who was likely screaming inside the camper while Mom was changing her diaper, and Dad had stepped away to one of our camping neighbor's sites to chat for a minute. And there I was, peering at the glowing light, on my own, without my mother's watchful eye and stern "Don't touch that!" I extended my left index finger and reached across the table toward the white light, protected by the glass domed lid. How hot could it be? I wondered. My young brain searched for a logical argument to support my actions—if the lantern were really that hot, surely those netted mantels inside the glass would burn to ashes? Inching closer to the glass, still unsupervised, curiosity surging through my tiny, five-year-old body, the tip of my left index finger, for the first and last time, made contact with our Coleman lantern.

"OUCH!" quickly followed by the scream for my "MOMMMMY!" and a waterfall of tears and cries immediately ensued. Mom burst out of the camper and my father ran back to our campsite to discover my error and injury. It was easy for them to discern what had happened as I held my left index finger out to them yelling "OUCH!" and "IT HURTS!" between my heaving sobs.

Mom and Dad simultaneously sprang into action. Mom scooped me up and carried me inside the camper to hold me and take a closer look at my finger. Dad made a bee line for the ice chest and broke off a few small chunks from our ice block and wrapped them in plastic wrap before returning to the camper. I was slow to be comforted and was convinced that the ice would make my finger hurt more. Dad reassured me that the ice would make the burning stop, while Mom stroked my hair and gently rocked me.

Only after I was tucked into my sleeping bag that night, my eyes puffy and red from crying, with my throbbing left index finger resting on a fresh pouch of ice did my mother remind me of her warning. "I told you not to touch that, Sheri! The lantern gets very hot and see what happened? It burned you." I never forgot that lantern burn, and heeded my mother's wise and stern advice (about the lantern anyway) from that night forward.

Pebble to Ponder

My Coleman lantern experience illustrates how our lives are guided and shaped by following or not following principles. From family dynamics to corporate drama, principles are fundamental, trusted truths that without emotional bias contribute to our success or justify our failings. Although everyone was upset that night along Alpine Creek when I burned my finger on the Coleman, the principle held true—touch the lantern, it will burn you. The lantern didn't care that I was curious or that I searched for a logical explanation to justify my actions. The lantern followed the scientific principles of heat and burns. The lantern followed the rules for principles.

Principles are accepted rules. Pay taxes, obey speed limits or risk a ticket, don't cheat on school tests. We grow up learning to follow the rules. We do what is expected in society, at work, and in our families. When we follow the rules, we are usually rewarded with a calm and predictable life. When we break the rules and rebel, we are usually held accountable and punished with either natural (getting burned) or agreed upon (speeding ticket) consequences.

Principles are fundamental, primary truths. Our physical world is governed by fundamental, primary truths. Principles that are reliable operate flawlessly and seemingly effortlessly. Water runs downstream. Lightening is attracted to water. The sun rises in the east and sets in the west.

Principles are based on belief. Sometimes principles center on things we are taught in school or at church or as part of our corporate cultures. We may believe such principles are based on the experience of others, or interpretation of scripture, or job title. Do unto others. Turn the other cheek. Honesty is the best policy. Your mother is always right. Sales always slump in the summer.

Principles are personal. After sifting though all the rules, fundamental truths and beliefs, we settle on our personal set of principles. Rules we choose to follow. The codes we live our life by. We decide which principles are more important than others—which hills we are willing to die on, and which rules, with justifiable cause can be bent.

As human beings, we've all experienced Coleman lantern examples of testing a principle and finding ourselves stung and burned. Pushing against the limits, and testing motherly warnings is how we develop our own guiding set of rules we each live by. On the flip side, holding fast to a set of personal principles, even when our world spins out of our control, can help us feel grounded, connected, and safe. And in most cases, at the end of the day, we can argue that Mom, indeed, is always right.

The see-saw challenge at Fallen Leaf Lake

PROFICIENCY
Waves and Waterskiing

Nothing great was ever accomplished without enthusiasm.
—Ralph Waldo Emerson

The mirror-smooth water of Fallen Leaf Lake beckons the waterskiing enthusiast to show off. In the peak summer months when water temperatures rose above frigid, the sound and sight of speed boats towing hot-dogging waterskiers right past Sherman Cabin, were an early-morning delight. I loved the way the lake looked just before the sun peaked out over Lookout Ridge. The reflection of the pine trees and mountains surrounding the lake offered the perfect, unspoiled identical twin image in the water.

"Smooth as glass," my mother would say and she'd peer wistfully out of the cabin windows hoping to spot a brave water-skier. In her youth, Mom had been a proficient water skier—it was her badge of sporting competence. She bore a battle wound from her early years of extreme sporting, a scar on the underside of her left elbow from where she'd had surgery after breaking her arm attempting to ski into the shore to impress her comrades. The injury, coupled with age, made Mom the perfect waterskiing fan, and from the safe distance of the Sherman Cabin porch, or standing near the railing at the lodge store, Mom admired and analyzed the Fallen Leaf Lake skiers.

In the years before our upgrade to Sherman Cabin, we alternated our lakeside water play between the public swimming dock and a small children's beach by the boat rental marina. I preferred the water by the swimming dock, but for all-day picnics and water toys and playing in the sand, the area by the boat rental marina was clearly superior. Here Diana and I could build castles in the sand, and Mom, with her crochet project in her lap, could keep a close eye on us from the comfort of her folding chair in the shade on the beach. And, because most of the speed boats started and ended their thrill rides from the marina area, Mom enjoyed an unobstructed vantage point from which to watch the waterskiers.

As a young girl, I didn't like the ski boats. They were noisy and created lots of waves that would ripple toward the shore in rapid succession, destroying a sand creation built too close to the water, and causing me to bounce and tilt on my blue-and-white, polka-dot inflatable raft. The feeling of unsteadiness as I floated on top of the water freaked me out. I felt out of control, out of my element, and unsure what to do should a huge wave cause my little raft to capsize.

As I grew and became a more adept swimmer, the waves kicked up by the speed boats didn't bother me. The waves near our dock at Sherman Cabin were steady every afternoon from a combination of the churn of speedboats and the afternoon breezes sweeping down from Desolation Wilderness. I learned that the waves were nothing to be afraid of, and as my water skills and strength improved, so did my ability to work with the waves rather than be freaked out by them.

Diana and I invented game a game called "See-Saw" where we would sit facing each other on top of an oversized truck inner tube, locking our feet on the opposite underside of the tube for balance. The goal of the game was to rock the inner tube up and down (like a see-saw), creating waves and attempt to knock each other off the tube. The winner was the one who managed to stay perched on the tube, while the loser ended up in the water. We'd play this game for hours upon hours in the late afternoon, and loved when waterskiers added more challenge to our game by providing us with stronger, boat-generated waves.

We became experts at knowing how to combine the force of our see-saw rocking with the oncoming ripples of the boat waves. We learned the best angles for dumping the other into the water. We learned how to better balance on the tube when the boat waves hit. And we learned that when the tube capsized and one (or both) of us ended up in the lake, that the water provided a soft and safe landing, and that we'd float back above the surface quickly.

Each day as the afternoon sun faded into dusk and the inner tubes were tied up with sturdy ropes, the waves and boats and waterskiers dispersed for the night. The lake became quiet again and the water returned to its "smooth as glass" state until well after dawn the next day, when the whole cycle of waves and proficient recreation would begin again.

Pebble to Ponder

Doing your best at whatever you do is a simple way to describe proficiency. From doing the laundry to waterskiing to designing corporate strategic plans, proficiency is a defining characteristic of success. Being competent and proficient carries, along with the satisfaction of a job well done, the confidence to tackle larger projects or more daring feats. Becoming proficient often includes a long-term pursuit, working to master one or more of the following dimensions.

Training. Water skiing, building a computer, or teaching a class of feisty sixth graders, requires more than sheer desire or common sense knowledge gained by everyday living. In order to contribute our best in these types of activities, we must be willing to seek learning and the tricks of the trade to realize success. Being taught principles and techniques by those who are already proficient and adopting the best practices they share, put us on the road to proficiency.

Practice. Competence comes from believing and knowing we can do something well because we've exhibited a track record of doing it well. From making a prized lasagna to navigating boat waves on an inner tube, to presenting to the board of directors, the more we repeat a task and refine our methods, the more proficient we become. Through repetition, we discover short cuts and better ways to reach our desired results.

Challenge. As human beings, we constantly seek improvement—to better our best, to reach a little farther today than we did yesterday. So once we become expertly proficient at something, our sense of satisfaction is usually coupled with a desire to branch out in a new direction or add to our ever growing list of triumphs and accomplishments. Using waterskiing as an example, most folks who make this sport a hobby begin by becoming comfortable on two skis, then learn to slice effortlessly from side to side on just one ski. Life-long skiing enthusiasts don't seem satisfied to stop once they become an expert with just one ski and tricks, jumps, spins and other water acrobatics often become part of their proficient ski routines.

Doing what we do well, being proficient, requires that we not let up on our on our training, practice, and new challenges. If we allow ourselves to get rusty, to think we don't require practice or constant training, we will find that our level of expertise and competence also suffers. While we might not forget how to ride our bike, the first ride after a long winter sabbatical may leave us feeling a little less confident as we pedal. The same is true for most things in life. Only by continuing to DO what we do well will we feel confident when the speed boat waves catch us off guard and bounce and tilt us on our blue-and-white, polka-dot, inflatable rafts.

Spectacular view of the Falls

PONDERINGS
Fires and Flashlights

The day, water, sun, moon, night—
I do not have to pay to enjoy these things.
—Titus Maccius Platus

We loved the long summer days and lingering twilight at Fallen Leaf Lake. As the warmth of the summer sun faded, we waited to spot the first star as it glowed into view in the darkening sky. Before long, the deep violet sky filled with thousands of brilliant stars, so many more than we could see in the sky over our city home. Sounds of power boats and splashing in the water were also slowly replaced by the song of crickets and the crackle of campfires.

Our family friends, Rod and Jesse Boyer, rented a small one-bedroom cabin every summer at Fallen Leaf Lake. Their small cabin, *Eagle's Eyrie*, sat high on a hillside overlooking the campground near Alpine Creek. One of my favorite nighttime activities was to spend the evening at Rod and Jesse's place eating an open-fire-cooked meal and enjoying a warm, crackling campfire.

Rod, an easy-going, always calm, very tall and lanky police officer from southern California knew how to make the thickest, most flavorful hamburgers I'd ever tasted. While Rod built a fire fit for roasting the beef, his wife Jesse made comforting side dishes and sliced the lettuce, tomatoes and cheese, while Diana and I set the outdoor dining table. The relaxing meal against the backdrop of mountain evening sounds and dimming light created a magical ambience.

After dinner, Diana and I would follow Dad and Rod back down to the fire pit and watch as they built up the flames again by adding logs to the cooking fire. We'd pull the green-painted rattan chairs close to the fire, and on cool nights, we'd fetch a couple of thick, wool blankets from the cabin before settling in for the after-dinner entertainment. Once settled, we'd laugh and recall the adventures of our vacation, while Rod would whittle something interesting from a stick with his pocket knife. Mom and Jesse would talk about Avon cosmetics or the elementary school library where Jesse worked, while Diana and I would sit and listen with rapt attention to the soothing adult conversation, waiting for the fire to burn down once more to glowing, marshmallow-roasting coals.

Diana and I knew our only chance to roast marshmallows was at Rod Boyer's fire. Dad liked roaring campfires with tall flames; patiently waiting for a fire to burn down to glowing coals was not his forte. Rod's style, on the other hand, mirrored a slow-burning campfire; we could tell he enjoyed watching as the flames flickered and dimmed to reveal perfect roasting pockets of red orange. The hot, sweet, light brown, melted and crusty puffs of sugar were the perfect nightcap to an evening with Rod and Jesse.

By the time we were filled to the brim with the sticky sweets, the summer twilight had surrendered to the pitch-black mountain night. The thick darkness was only challenged by occasional firelight from other campsites or electric light filtering out from the cabins that lined the lake. Tearing ourselves away from the cozy light of the Boyer's meant switching to a different means of illumination—flashlights, to guide our way back down to the Lodge and along the road to Sherman Cabin.

The flashlights provided a very focused beam of light to ensure our safety as we walked along. Most often, I'd point my beam of light directly in front of me about two feet ahead. This gave me time to compensate if a rock or pothole popped into view. Sometimes my curiosity would beckon me to shine the light up on a hill or into a tree to spot a creature. Pointing the flashlight directly above my head yielded the least benefit as the beam would be swallowed by the night sky, disappearing against the brilliant display of stars above.

While the walk always seemed longer at night, eventually we'd arrive back at our cabin, climb the rocky path to the entry and switch from flashlight to electric lights, adding our cabin's flicker to the dozens of other homes and cabins that silently pushed against the mountain darkness.

Pebble to Ponder

Unlike the daytime recreational distractions, nighttime at Fallen Leaf provided hours of quieter time. Reflection, consideration, and creativity found the time and space to develop during those crackly, warm campfire circles and beam-led walks through the mountain darkness. The differing characteristics of these forms of light—firelight, flashlight and electric light—mirror the pondering thoughts nurtured on those summer nights.

The changing mood of our campfires, from tall bright flames to hot glowing coals, correlated to the changing moods of our thoughts. Certain issues, usually politically controversial in nature, would escalate the volume and intensity of the adult conversation around the Boyer's fire. While booming voices were unusual at Fallen Leaf, I knew that the oxygen feeding the flames of the fire and the flames of the conversation topic would soon die down—unless the fiery discussion received more fuel, more dry wood to burn. As the real fire burned and the flames flickered and dimmed, the adult conversation also became softer, with longer pauses in between comments as each of my adult role models quietly reflected on a burning issue in his or her mind, now merely simmering and glowing like the orange-red coals.

Sitting there, near the firelight, I'd let my eyes settle on the fire and become lost in the changing waves of the flames. The gentle hiss of the burning wood would sometimes be interrupted by the crackle of a spark. If the flames found a burning log covered in tree sap, the crackling would intensify and hot embers would pop and shoot out of the fire in rapid succession. These pops and crackles remind me of those flashes of inspiration or great ideas that surprise us when they appear in our minds out of nowhere. Often unrelated and random, these sparks can cause us to jump back and pause, and yet also, be the small glowing start of something great.

The light from a flashlight is much different, more focused, more intense. Unlike the burning heat of a glowing camp fire, the flashlight's purpose is to guide our steps and lead the way safely home. When our thoughts are focused on a single objective or goal, or when we are seeking to spot the familiar while surrounded in darkness, our pondering is more like the light of our flashlight.

Both firelight and flashlight need fuel to produce illumination. Wood and a spark, or a light bulb and batteries, combine to create ponderings and inspirational light.

Identifying and utilizing the tools and sources of fuel to feed our creativity and quiet time yield solutions through musing and illuminating reflection.

We all have periods when darkness crowds out the light in our lives or careers. These times can seem black and void of optimism or solutions. Answers sometimes come like a crackly spark from a fire. Other times, we find the warmth of hope in quiet, glowing reflection. Finally, the focused beam of deliberate action can lead us to our desired destination by pushing the darkness out of our way as we journey forward back to the electric light—trusted , steady and safe—of home.

The clouds move in over Fallen Leaf Lake

PROMISE
Thunderstorm

*Not everything that counts can be counted, and not everything
that can be counted counts.*
—Albert Einstein

*Faith is building on what you know is here so you can reach
what you know is there.*
—Cullen Hightower

On purpose, our family vacations to Fallen Leaf Lake were scheduled during a four-week window that pretty well guaranteed warm weather, blue skies, and very few clouds. While my father felt fairly confident in his ability to accurately predict the weather, every once in a while at our Tahoe paradise, his expertise failed him, and we woke to grey skies and a promise of thunderstorms. While certainly the exception rather than the rule, these days forced my sister and me to adjust our rigid outside plans and opt for lazy indoor activities of games, word puzzles, and afternoon naps. While we tried to accept the inevitability of the occasional storm, because we treasured each day in the outdoors of our lake, it was difficult to lose even one hour to foul weather. One of us always volunteered to keep a watchful vigil on the condition of the sky on these strange days, because we knew it was a simple matter of waiting—waiting for the promise of sunshine to return.

From the loft where my sister and I slept, I recall waking one morning to the rumble of thunder. As I gazed out over the treetops toward the lake, the water turned a milky-gray and the tree branches swayed vigorously in the wind. The leaves on the aspen trees also showed their silver underbellies in preparation for rain. The typical sounds of happy bird chirping were absent on this morning, as I imagined the stellar jays, chipmunks, and other small creatures taking cover from the pending downpour. As if on cue, the thunder clapped loudly, the skies opened, and hard, pelting raindrops began to dance on the roof, the deck, and the lake below. I looked at my sister with a little sadness in my face as we both realized this storm looked like it would last the entire day.

By lunch time, we'd played marathon games of *Aggravation* and *Pinochle*. Every few minutes, Diana or I would scramble to the window and look for signs of hope—parting clouds or to check the frequency/size of the raindrops. The rain was not slowing. The clouds were not parting. Our day seemed lost. We paused for lunch, working to keep stiff upper lips, and spent some time swinging in the indoor hammock that was mounted to the cabin's exposed support beams. If either of us heard what we thought was a break in the steady rain, we'd run to the window and inspect the sky. Mom offered to take us into town to seek something else to do while the rain persisted. Diana and I held our ground, certain that if we abandoned our watchful posts, the clouds would part and we would miss out on the remainder of the afternoon outdoors.

By 3 p.m., Mom and Dad were completely fed up with the cabin fever consuming my sister and me. With the rain still falling, that evening at dinner, my sister and I sat silently, all hope for time at the lake gone. The promise of sunlight had not been fulfilled.

Even as an adult, I obsess with the weather forecast. The promise of storms, or sun, or snow coupled with the complete LACK of control over the elements, often produces an off-balance feeling for me. One example in particular occurred a few years ago in early December as I attended a company meeting in Los Angeles. I left a cold and dreary Seattle to embrace clear, Southern California warmth, sporting short sleeves, sunglasses, and the anticipation of the sun's rays seeping into my skin to warm me from the inside out.

Back home, however things were not as tepid. The sky turned from grey to a dark slate and the wind began to howl in Maple Valley. The next morning, the storm continued to rage, leaving all of Maple Valley (and over 200,000 other homes in the Seattle area) without power. While I knew that my family was safe and staying with friends away from the house, I was obsessed with the storm and worried myself into a stupor. I listened to the Seattle public radio station from my laptop on every break at my meeting. I logged onto the Seattle Times newspaper and local news websites to get the latest information on the storm. I even called the 800 number for the power company by pressing Redial on my cell phone more than a few times, desperate for news that power had been restored.

I hate not being in control! I worried about trees falling into my roof or through my windows. I worried about the cats being cold and alone in the dark. I worried about the water freezing in the pipes and bursting, flooding the house. And all the while, worrying about what I could not change and could not control, I was not contributing anything positive to my business meeting.

I really needed to gain some perspective on this situation. So I put a call into a professional lifeline (a.k.a., career coach) and dumped out all I was feeling. She asked me three piercing questions:

1. What did I have to offer at this meeting in Los Angeles?
2. How was I accomplishing what I needed to at the meeting while worrying about what was happening at home?
3. Did I believe the storm would pass?

While it took a few minutes for the impact of those questions to sink in, I eventually stopped fretting about the water pipes freezing and the kitties shivering in the dark. I pulled myself back into the present and threw myself into the meeting, trusting that I would return home to find all was well. To find the storm had passed. To find the promise of spring just around the corner.

Pebble to Ponder

The promise of tomorrow casts an alluring spell on all of us. Being caught up in the future, the hazy horizon we cannot yet see clearly on our journey, is an easy outlet for our thoughts. It's easy to get pulled away from the present task by thinking about the future. One phone call from a client, friend or family member who is having a difficult time, can turn an otherwise productive and positive day dark and gloomy.

Some of my father's best advice to me as a young girl was: "Do what you need to do, when you need to do it—you're the only one who can." If not me, then who? If not now, then when?

When we wait for the storm to end, we miss out on the now. By worrying about freezing pipes bursting or a lost day of water play at Fallen Leaf Lake, I missed out on… well, I'll never know exactly what I missed out on, because I missed out on it! So, while we might not always be in control of the storms swirling around us—when they come, how long they last or the damage they do—we CAN be in control of how we react to them.

Do you believe the storm will pass? If so, trust that belief and get on with what you can accomplish despite the raging storm. If you don't believe the storm will pass, reach out to a "lifeline" and lean on his or her belief until you begin to accept the truth. The sun will always return when the storm has passed. I promise.

Soaking up the sun at Fallen Leaf Lake

PASSING IT ON
Red Convertible

The jump is so frightening between where I am and where I want to be. Because of all I may become I will close my eyes and leap!
—Mary Ann Radmaker

About one month into a new position in a new industry, still working on orienting myself to new processes, people, routines and my contributing role, I found myself on a small prop plane flying from Seattle, Washington to Billings, Montana. The purpose of my trip was to meet one of my top district leaders, a woman who carried considerable influence in the company and who enjoyed a thriving annual sales volume, a strong management team, and had numerous years of experience. In arranging the details of the visit by phone, Jan, her cheery voice helping to calm my nerves, offered to meet my flight at the airport and chauffer me to my hotel. Having never traveled to Billings, Montana before, I gratefully accepted her kind invitation.

Landing in Billings and realizing I had no idea what Jan looked like, I made my way through the small airport toward the escalators and baggage claim. As I began to scan the lobby area, I spotted Jan immediately—she was beaming in my direction. I walked directly up to Jan, extending my hand to offer a proper business handshake, and she surprised me by throwing her arms around me in a warm, welcoming hug, her kind voice echoing "We're so glad you are here, Sheryl." I immediately felt more relaxed.

Jan led me outside of the airport after collecting my bags, and my eyes began searching the parking lot for a car that would represent the level of success Jan enjoyed. As we walked, a classic red convertible popped into view and after a few more steps, it was obvious we were heading straight for it. "I brought the fancy convertible today—we save it for important occasions," Jan offered. Jan had left the top down so we tossed my luggage in the back seat and Jan invited me to hop in. She seemed so comfortable and content in her classic red convertible. She started the engine and pushed a cassette tape into the stereo and classic rock and roll began to play. I knew then I was in for an adventure.

I attempted a casual look at the sky. Montana is known as Big Sky Country, and on this particular day, the big sky was filled with big, tall, dark, thunderclouds. I decided not to worry, confident that if it began to rain, Jan would put the top back up as we continued on our journey to the heart of downtown Billings. Just as we exited the airport parking lot, hard, fat drops of warm water began to fall. Surely, Jan will stop and put the top up—she won't want to mess up her hair/makeup/outfit for our meeting. The drops began falling faster, and with the top still down, Jan looked over and smiled: "You aren't afraid of a little rain, are you, Sheryl?"

We drove through downtown Billings in the rain, with the top down and Jan pointed out various sites. And actually, the rain felt nicely refreshing as it landed on my face and arms as we journeyed along. Attempting to change the subject from the weather, I asked: "So, Jan how long have you owned this great convertible?"

Her face lit up and she replied enthusiastically, "Owning this car was one of my fifty goals and dreams. An exercise the company asked us to do before a big director meeting years ago was to write a list of 50 of our goals and dreams and bring them with us to the meeting. Do you have a list of 50 goals and dreams, Sheryl?"

I'll admit I was intrigued with the question and the concept of such a list. Unfortunately, as I took a mental inventory of my "goals," I stopped counting before I reached ten. I invited Jan to tell me more, and the lesson I learned that day from our drive in the red convertible with the top down in the rain, remains a key touchstone for me.

By the time I completed my visit to Billings, Jan had me promise her I would complete my list of 50 goals and dreams that very day, on the plane ride home. I agreed.

I found the experience of writing the list much more challenging than it sounded. How hard could it be to write a list of 50 dreams? As I began, the first ten or so items read like a to-do list.

- Hire a gardener.
- Achieve/maintain ideal weight. Be physically fit !!!!
- New countertops in kitchen.

After item #10, I found myself stuck, tapping my pencil on the paper and thinking, "What else do I want to do?" By the time the little prop plane landed in Seattle, my list only contained 16 items. I folded the paper, and placed it in my day planner and forgot my promise for a couple of weeks.

A reminder of my commitment to complete my list of 50 goals and dreams arrived about two weeks later in the mail with a card from Jan. The hand-written message inside jolted me into new resolve:

> Dear Sheryl,
>
> Thank you for your visit to Billings! You passed the test! You didn't let a little rain with the top down spoil your mood. Have you finished your list of 50 goals and dreams? Opportunities will present themselves in the most amazing ways once you have written down your dreams.
>
> Love you, Jan

I fished around in my planner for the folded sheet of paper where I'd begun my list, cleared away some of the mounting clutter on my desk and began to think again. I reviewed what I had written, and it somehow seemed so generic. My eyes traveled to my bookcase and a title jumped out at me from one of the spines: "Re-imagine!"

I let my mind go, and began to re-imagine my dreams—the most outrageous, crazy dreams I could think of, and began writing. My list began to take on a dynamic dimension and new ideas sprung from words I'd just written. My list wasn't filling with to-do's but with possibilities. It was laden with belief and hope, rather than skepticism and fear. When I put my pencil down this time, my list contained 60 items.

Pebble to Ponder

It wasn't like I doubted Jan when she said that "Opportunities would present themselves in amazing ways" once I'd written my list of dreams. She had shared with me (by citing the number on her list) how she had found ways to fulfill her dreams simply by having them written down and planted in her mind and heart. She shared she was able to recognize opportunities that may have otherwise gone unnoticed. Once, Jan had re-called, she was irritated with pot holes in her street and called the Billings City Hall to complain. The unexpected answer from the voice on the other end, "Well, perhaps you should consider running for City Council so you can fix the problem" helped Jan fulfill one of her dreams to become more involved in local government. (She filled two terms on the Billings City Council.)

More than five years have flown by since I composed my list. I've re-written the list and recorded it in a journal I carry with me in my laptop bag. I pull the list out regularly and review it. Many items remain untouched and out there in What-was-I thinking-land: "#19: Be invited to the White House" and "#55: Have a private lunch/conversation with Hillary Clinton" fall in this category.

Others, like "#2: Write a book," are actually happening—with steady progress being made to achieve them. As if by magic, several others are being accomplished in unexpected ways. For example, significant progress on "#7: Be physically fit and maintain a healthy weight!!!" came through my triathlon experience, which you've already read about. With each passing year, as I review my list, make creative edits, and cast my intention in the direction of my dreams, more and more will continue to be fulfilled.

Jan saw an opportunity to pass on a lesson that had helped her reach the success she enjoyed and she freely shared it without fear or hesitation. While not complete strangers, having not met me, she still took a chance to share her wisdom without thoughts of rejection or reproach.

Passing on our successes, best practices, and life insights is a gift we can choose to give freely to those around us. Life can become a bleak routine of survival and we can become stuck in the motions of working, paying the bills, working more, paying more bills. Remembering to dream, to cast away difficult realities and focus on awesome possibilities, is a gift we can give to ourselves, our families, and those we work with and touch in the world.

As artist and writer Mary Anne Radmaker states: "The jump is so frightening between where I am and where I want to be. Because of all I may become, I will close my eyes and leap!" Why not reach out and share those golden gems of insight as easily as we share a movie recommendation? Why not pass our dreams forward and transfer the art of dreaming to everyone we touch, even while driving in the rain with the top down in a classic red convertible?

PERSPECTIVE
Eyes of the Heart

We are what we think. All that we are arises with our thoughts.
With our thoughts, we make the world.
—Buddha

Spring is my second favorite season, next to the sun and warmth of summer. I love spring for all of the typical reasons—new growth, vibrant colors, the predictable return of the chickadees and house finches, the sweet twilight of longer days. I love how spring recharges my resolve and determination. It's as if the winter's hold on the earth and my heart both melt away together.

In May 2008, I climbed into a rental car in Reno, Nevada, and like a returning chickadee, made my way through Carson City, and up the steep and winding Highway 50 to my Fallen Leaf Lake paradise.

The anticipation continues to mount as I climb higher and higher, my ears popping as the car reaches Spooner Summit and Lake Tahoe explodes into view. The sight takes my breath away and I gasp as the blue sky reflects on the unmistakable blue water of Lake Tahoe. For a moment, my eyes stray to the mountains in the distance to my left and I think, "Paradise is just over there."

Many of the stores and hotels and restaurants I remember from childhood still line highways 50 and 89 from Zephyr Cove to Camp Richardson. I smile as I pass them and memories of renting bicycles, eating Mexican food, or staying at the Motel 6 one winter weekend splash me in the face. It's still pre-season, so the campground at Camp Richardson is deserted and the ice cream parlor and pack station where we'd saddle up each summer for a trail ride on horseback haven't opened yet. My heart jumps into my throat as the small green sign "Fallen Leaf Lake: 5 miles" marks the familiar left turn from the well-maintained Highway 89 to Fallen Leaf's infamous road.

Suddenly, without any warning, I am crying.

It is a cool, spring day, but the mix of sun and white fluffy clouds beckon me to roll down the window. I turn the radio off. I creep along, tears streaming down my face as I am overtaken by each detail of my surroundings. The smell of the fragrant pines. Chipmunks perched on sunny, speckled granite rocks. Wild flowers and new spring grass flutter in the meadow with still snow-topped peaks of Mount Cathedral and Mount Tallac welcoming me home. The birds sing to me, alerting the forest that I am here. I am home.

My eyes begin to take in the changes as well. New cabins and homes have sprung up alongside the veteran cottages I remember with their intricate hand-carved, roadside plaques marking the addresses. Forest fires have claimed many trees, as has clearing for new construction. When I arrive at the parking spot near the huge boulder marking Sherman Cabin, I find it much changed as well. New owners have put their name on the address plaque. A new private swim/boat dock stands beneath me on the lakeshore. The dirt path that led up the hill to the cabin has been updated with rock steps, accent lighting, and a sturdy railing. From the road, I gaze up at the cabin and while the general structure is the same, the faded and creaky wrap-around porch I remember has been modernized.

Fallen Leaf Lodge has changed as well. The old store still stands watch lakeside, but is not used. A new building houses the store, gift shop, and grill that serves delicious sandwiches and hamburgers. Original stoneware from the coffee shop and other memorabilia are for sale in the new store. The public swimming dock—my pebble-collecting home-base—is now part of a private collection of homes and condominiums that are part of the Fallen Leaf Home Owners Association.

I park the car and walk along the lakefront, past the old store and swim dock. Things have changed. I am walking on what used to be the public road leading to Lily Lake and the Glen Alpine Trail Head. It's quieter now, and sand covers what used to be a rocky, asphalt, one-lane road. I wind up the hill away from the lake and notice more new homes where the Lodge's rental cabins once stood.

Things have changed. At the fork in the road near the little church at the head of what used to be the campground along the creek, stands the a new Fallen Leaf Lake Fire Department building. I walk ahead, my heart heavy as I pass through the deserted campground, and site of our family's first upgrade from tent to cabin life, Cathedral View. The cabin is gone, the rocky remains of the foundation are its only evidence. As I turn right and begin to climb the last hill before reaching my destination, the springtime roar of the lower falls fills my ears to bursting.

I am standing on the edge of a familiar steep and rocky overlook and the lower falls in all their glory sing to me: "Welcome Home." The sky is beyond brilliant and as I gaze up, Mount Cathedral smiles down at me. "I'm still here," it whispers on a cool sierra breeze that fills the canyon and follows the creek all the way to the lake. "What matters is still here." New, hot tears spill over onto my cheeks. I am home.

I stay here, my feet glued to this spot, at the falls. I listen to the familiar roar, mesmerized by the falling water, the blue sky, and the immense presence of Mount Cathedral. And for a moment, as I take in this place, untouched by years, by change, by the evidence of man, I hear my mother's voice calling her familiar "Yoo-hoo!" I see my father attempting to cross the roaring stream below to stand nearer to the falls, and I imagine my sister and me playing on the sunny rocks at the base of the falls. Here, in this place, for the briefest moment, nothing has changed.

I finally tear myself away from my imaginings, and begin the walk back downhill toward the lake and my waiting car. Along my return path, I notice the details that remain unchanged—like the wild blackberry bushes growing right off the path at the little church, the small stones that blend with the asphalt of this narrow road, and the way Fallen Leaf Lake bursts into view as I make the last curving descent past the cabins. Mount Cathedral, now at my back, continues to whisper comforting words through the pine trees, "What matters is still here. What is most important hasn't changed."

My stride back toward the store is lighter and filled with satisfaction. I am surrounded by memories of sounds, smells, voices, and random moments from the thousands of hours spent at Fallen Leaf Lake. And while I cannot deny the evidence of change that has occurred here, I am suddenly struck by the obvious truth that I have changed as well. I have grown from a small girl who truly believed the pebbles at the lake held gold, to a woman who searches for meaning in the pebbles of life's experiences. My long pigtails of pre-adolescence, care-free days spent in the blazing sun without SPF-50 lotion, and worries no larger than how long the weather will hold, are long gone. I have changed.

Days, years, and decades have all left their mark. My winding and sometimes unclearly marked career path, my journey to find peace and love, and a personal battle to stay healthy and fit, have all contributed important lessons and pebbles on my journey. Dreams and goals, what-if's and uh-oh's collect in my mind's eye and the image of a shoreline of my life's pebbles settles in my heart.

As I reach the rental car, I pause before pulling out and continuing on my journey—back to Reno, back home to Seattle, and back to whatever lies in store. I fix the immortal images of my paradise, my Fallen Leaf Lake, in my heart—the sky, the water, the trees, my mountain—and take in a deep, satisfying breath. No matter where my journey leads, my Fallen Leaf Lake home will always stand here, waiting, beckoning, offering the lessons of the pebbles.

Pebble to Ponder

"With our thoughts, we make the world." What we think about shapes our journey in life—both in our families and relationships and in our career. Thanks to the success of *The Secret*, we've learned about the power of intention—what we think about happens. From corporate quotas to paying our bills, we are all the sum of what we think about. For many, negative images and messages have become such a habit or focal point that attracting anything positive is difficult. Then there are the blind optimists, who see opportunity in everything and never seem to have a bad day. The rest of us live somewhere in between.

It's not just what we think about that makes our world, but WHEN we think about. We spend too much time in the past, and get frustrated when life or work isn't the same as it used to be. We beat ourselves (and our teams) up for not hitting targets. We relive our mistakes and regrets over and over and over. Our heart does not easily let go of our shortcomings.

We also spend too much time thinking about the future. Deciding we will be happy once we have $250,000 in our savings account. Or the job of our dreams. Or a happy, peaceful relationship. Or health. While I'm not suggesting there's no use in planning or setting goals—LIVING in the future, in our minds, causes us to miss out on the wonderful and opportunity-laden now.

I think what the Buddha meant by "with our thoughts, we shape the world" is what we think about in the PRESENT. How we take the lessons and wonder and beauty that exists today and think on that. How on purpose, we take action, consistent and persistent action, every day, toward our dreams. By thinking in the present about the present, we shape our world, our journey, day by day.

The pebbles I collected at Fallen Leaf Lake are a treasure as valuable and price-less as an antique family heirloom. I carry the pebbles with me wherever I go. Their lessons inspire me, guide me, remind me of important relationships and principles.

And so it is for all of us. We each have a beach lined with the pebbles that make up our lives, our memories, our treasures.

The pebbles are here. All around us. Pick one up. Bring the lessons from the pebbles into the present. Allow your collection of pebbles to guide and remind you of important lessons. Listen to the pebbles promptings and take determined action in the direction of your dreams.

Epilogue
Miracles Happen

What we have once enjoyed we can never lose...
All that we love deeply becomes a part of us.
—Helen Keller

Faded photographs and a portrait that hung just inside the doorway to my parents' bedroom were the only evidence of him. My father's wistful stares and occasional unexplained sadness confused and bothered me, and the topic of the young boy pictured on the wall was rarely discussed. My older brother was lost to me from just after my birth until January 2008. We've spent the last year becoming best friends, reconnecting the dots of our histories and our lives. The miracle of our reunion seems a fitting way to end this collection of inspirational stories.

My big brother John was the apple of my father's eye. They wore matching shirts and my dad even cut John's hair to match his own military flat top. As sometimes sadly happens, my father's marriage to John's mother ended in divorce. When John's mom decided to re-marry, my father gave up his parental rights so John could be adopted by his new step-father. John grew up in Concord, California and for a time, lived just three streets over from my childhood home. Even after he moved to another part of town for his high school years, he kept tabs on us—occasionally driving past our home on Wilson Lane to try to catch a glimpse of his dad or the sisters he didn't know.

The absence of John in our lives, through all the years of our family vacations to Fallen Leaf Lake and milestones of growing up, loomed like a cloud over Dad's head. Not having contact with his son became a life-long regret, and as my sister and I grew into adults and came to understand more of the specifics around our brother's absence, we also wondered where he was and what he was doing with his life. "I wouldn't know little John if he walked up to me on the street," became Dad's heartbreaking refrain.

In 2007, my family was blessed with a miracle. Mom had been gone for a little over three years, and healing came slowly for all of us. Dad, while holding onto our home on Wilson Lane as long as he could, had moved into an assisted living facility and was experiencing health and financial issues that worried my sister and me.

Independent of this, my brother had been sorting through his mother's personal items and memorabilia after she had passed away, and wrestled with thoughts of finding Dad. John's curiosity was piqued, as was the desire to reconnect with the father he had known as a young boy. John wasn't sure if he would be welcomed or shunned. He assembled a box of memorabilia saved by his mother, put the box in the trunk of his car, and waited for a quiet voice of inspiration.

John's wife, Suzanne, provided regular prodding, knowing instinctively that not knowing was worse than any reaction he may receive. I am convinced that my mother also had a hand in these events. She also adored my brother John, and after several miscarriages and against her doctor's advice, had successfully given birth to me. Wanting so badly to be a mother, she had relished time with John. Dad recalled they were good buddies—and that the heartache of separation also weighed heavily on her. And so, I believe my mother whispered to my brother's heart: "Go find your dad—he needs your help."

One warm spring day, while driving through Concord with Suzanne, John found himself on Wilson Lane, driving up to our family home. The new owner greeted him and gave him the news that Dad had moved, gladly providing the address. I'm sure John's heart pounded fiercely as he approached the front lobby of the assisted living home. Still unsure how he would be received, he left the memorabilia box with the receptionist, giving a short explanation and leaving his phone number, "…if he wants to call me." The teary and miraculous father-and-son reunion that happened that very night has forever changed the make-up of my family.

My sister and I have a big brother! He is the perfect complement to the two of us—his easy-going nature, quick wit, and generous heart have brought healing and hope to our family. My father looks at his son with pride and love and gratitude—lifelong regret replaced with a twinkle in his eye. My loyal brother and my new sister, Suzanne, provide selfless care and daily visits with Dad. While Dad's health is declining, my sister and I know Dad's well-being is steadfastly watched over by our brother.

As I re-read this collection of memories, I am struck with a chord of sadness that John wasn't part of their creation—I can't help but wonder how events would have changed had he been with us each summer on our Fallen Leaf Lake getaways. The sadness fades though as I daydream about all the memories we have yet to create with John—a lifetime of experiences and pebbles yet to be uncovered.

I wake frequently with a smile on my face as I think of my big brother John, his protective and selfless love, and there isn't a doubt in my heart: miracles happen!

Reunion, July 2008: Diana, John and Sheri

PART THREE:
The P.O.W.E.R. Formula:
A guide for leadership and life™

There are only two feelings. Love and fear. There are only two
languages. Love and fear. There are only two activities. Love and
fear. There are only two motives, two procedures, two
frameworks, two results. Love and fear. Love and fear.
—Leunig

Trusting Math

I believe our lives are gifts meant to bless others. I believe each of us is unique, possessing skills and talents and a signature all our own. We are here to stamp our unique contribution on our world (lower case w) and by doing so, bless the World (upper case w) and leave it better for our being here. Our world (lower case w) includes all the people we touch, the lives we impact through our direct connections, the loves we share, the work we do.

Filmmaker Frank Capra wisely stated: "Every man is born with a inner capacity to take him as far as his imagination can dream or envision."

Homemaker, Avon lady, travel agent, and my beloved mother, Shirley Hughey said often: "You can accomplish anything you set your mind to." Whatever our lot, luck or position, our job is to find our gifts, develop our talents, stamp our signature on our actions, and go about the business of blessing others. By doing so, we create our legacy for our World (upper case W).

We enter the World not knowing how we will serve it. When we are true to our unique purpose, we leave the World knowing we have served it.

I believe in formulas and roadmaps and signs to aid us in our quest to live the contributing lives we are meant to live. While math has never been my forte, I believe in the basic concepts of addition, subtraction, multiplication, and division as they relate to our discovery and the implementation of our talents.

Synergy is created through addition. $1 + 1 = 3$. I believe success feeds on itself to generate more success—like fire feeds on fire. When two small flames join together, they feed on each other and create a hotter, brighter flame. When we add our efforts to the flames of others, our passion ignites and brightens our effectiveness.

Awareness of what we need to subtract is also vital to our success formula. What must I take away, or cease from doing/being, to excel in my contribution? $5 + 1 - 2 = 4$. Lets be honest, none of us walks a perfect road. We must be willing to identify those habits, actions, or perspectives that do not serve us. The heavy baggage of hurts, anger, pain and physical addictions make our loads heavier than they need to be. We must be willing to subtract them from our lives and let them go.

Embracing and working from our areas of strength allow us to multiply our influence and results. $5 \times 5 = 25$. It's not that we ignore the areas of opportunity—they are wellsprings of growth and expansion. In searching for our signature contribution, however, working from our strengths will generate momentum and propel us forward, multiplying our results.

Division. The most difficult equation to master. $100 / 25 = 4$. How do I divide my time, energy, heart, and passion among various priorities? Which comes first? How do I divide and not lose the benefit and strength that come from these important competing priorities? How do I throw myself equally into these various quadrants and not sacrifice quality? How much is too much division?

The basics of mathematical formulas: addition, subtraction, multiplication, and division serve as the foundation for developing our signature contribution. Another critical element is power. With more than 30 possible definitions, power means: the ability to do or act, a person who exercises influence, and energy, force, momentum. To accomplish anything we set our mind to requires power. The following roadmap introduces key elements of the P.O.W.E.R. Formula ™ for Leadership and Life.

(Templates for all activities are available for free download at www.thepowerofpebbles.com. Simply click on the resources page.)

P = Purpose

One of my favorite definitions of purpose comes from a scene in the second *Matrix* movie, *Matrix Revolutions*. The evil Agent Smith and the hero, Neo, are having a conversation on a basketball court about the purpose of living. Right before a brilliant slow motion fight scene in true Matrix style, Mr. Smith eloquently states:

> *There's no escaping reason, no denying purpose - because as we*
> *both know, without purpose, we would not exist. It is purpose*
> *that created us, purpose that connects us, purpose that pulls us,*
> *that guides us, that drives us, It is purpose that defines, Purpose*
> *that binds us.*

Ah, Hollywood.

Our purpose, our vision, our dream is our contribution. Each one of us has a purpose bigger than what we do for a living. Most of us find the task of discovering our clarity of purpose, our dream, our connection, happens in bits and pieces rather than as a single event. After all, most of us don't consult with the Oracle to be told our purpose is to save the world, as happened to Neo in *The Matrix*.

I've always been a bit jealous of great musicians or artists—their purpose is so obvious, so clear, so tangible. Discovering our own individual purpose often requires more than a scant attempt at introspective soul searching. Like looking through a pair of binoculars at a distant vista, our purpose becomes more clear, focused, and vibrant as we adjust the knobs.

Becoming clear on our purpose is an essential first step to claiming our P.O.W.E.R. There are no shortcuts. Discovering/ clarity of purpose requires that we spend time thinking, asking, processing, and refining our goals. It means daring to dream bigger and more audacious dreams than we may think we deserve. As our purpose evolves and grows, we begin to be fueled by our connection to it. We know we have found our purpose when that connection becomes so strong that obstacles, setbacks, failures, or sabotage cannot weaken our resolve.

Activities to Clarify Purpose

1. 50 GOALS and DREAMS

Make a list of 50 goals and dreams and review it at least once a month. Take the lid off your box and create a list of dreams—as if anything were possible. Don't limit your thinking. No idea is too crazy. Try to avoid making a "to-do" list.

2. THE ONE-HOUR GIFT

Give yourself (or your team) the gift of 1 hour of uninterrupted time to reflect on your purpose. No cell phones, laptops, or interruptions! Just quiet, reflective time. Ask yourself and journal your responses:

- What do I really, really, really want?
- What resources do I require?
- What obstacles stand in my way and how can I move forward in spite of them?
- What is the first step I will take today?

3. CHANGE YOUR wORLD AND THE WORLD

Divide a piece of paper into two columns. Make a list of ten or more ways you can change your wORLD (lower case w) down the left column of the paper. Your wORLD (lower case w) includes all the people you touch, the lives you impact through direct connections, the loves you share, the work you do. So consider how your direct contact and efforts can change your wORLD. In the right column, list impacts/contribution on the WORLD (upper case w) these changes could have. This takes some creative "bigger than me" thinking. Consider the far-reaching consequences and possibilities your efforts will have ten, fifty, one hundred years from now. How will fulfilling your purpose leave the WORLD a better place for you having served it?

4. BACK TO ART CLASS

Take a journey into the creative side of your mind. Get out construction paper, old magazines, stickers, glue, tape, crayons and markers and create a visual representation of your purpose. Find photos or headlines in magazines to add specific images and words to your purpose creation. Draw! Pick colors that represent your dreams. Share your purpose creation with your team or family. Mount it on a wall you see every day to remind your heart of your purpose.

5. LAST LECTURE

Imagine you are a college professor just prior to your retirement. Prepare your last lecture. What would you say to your students? What would you like them to remember from you as they continued on their journeys? If the image of public speaking and standing in front of a packed auditorium of students sounds intimidating, consider drafting a letter you'd leave to your family, the lessons or messages you'd like to leave for them to ease and aid them on their journey through life after you are no longer here.

O = Options

I freely admit I take comfort in a predictable routine or set of expectations in every area of my life from work, to family to recreation. I like to know what's coming, what to expect. But it's more than that. It's more about the feeling of comfortable competence and ease that accompanies routine. Feeling in control—certain that the lasagna will turn out as tasty as the last time or feeling competent that business coaching steps will lead to tangible success of the leader I'm working with—that kind of predictability. Who am I kidding? Our world doesn't seem to do routine much anymore, so being able to cope with change charging at us at the speed of light is a pre-requisite for EVERYTHING. To be able to cope with change, to realize true P.O.W.E.R., we must recognize and expand our options.

As comforting as it can be to follow the same route to and from work, allowing us the ease of autopilot, the comfort can be replaced by the exhilaration of finding an alternate route that saves time or gasoline or provides a more pleasing landscape. Staying fresh, being open to exploring new ideas, new ways of doing things, or taking risks, are all examples of expanding our options. Magic happens when we remain flexible and open to those alternate routes—more options, more ideas, more new ways of doing present themselves. I could list numerous examples of insurmountable obstacles, problems, plummeting results/sales, loss of key personnel, that have been overcome and solved by welcoming options in my own life. To drive the point home, here's one of my favorite option stories.

On a September morning in 1989, I walked into my first class as a graduate student in the College of Communications at Brigham Young University. The classroom on the second floor (underground) in the Harris Fine Arts Building boasted no windows, one door and a smattering of desks arranged in a semi-circle. At the head of the barren, beige painted classroom, a single table with a table top lectern and dust covered blackboard with chalk and an eraser completed the classrooms amenities. There were nine of us in the classroom—all eagerly awaiting the start of an exciting journey.

The professor strolled into the room, placed a book on the front table, pulled up a chair, and sat down. His first words to our class sent me into a spiral. "Welcome to Graduate School. There are nine of you now. By December, there will be five of you left. Two of you will finish this degree. That's the reality of what you are beginning today." I was devastated. My heart sank. How could I be one of only two graduates—how could I compete and succeed with so many other, more talented students in my class? My initial reaction was that I would not be among the two to finish. That night in my apartment I cried and felt sorry for myself and became trapped with the notion that I could not succeed against such odds. I could see no options.

As I ate my Cheerios the next morning, my gloomy mood continued, and I thought—why even bother going to class? I began to consider what I might do instead of going to class, instead of pursuing this degree. I began to look at options. I began to think about where I saw myself five years down the road. I began to consider the doors this degree would open for me in my career. I soon became lost among all the options swirling around in my head.

Before finishing my breakfast, I embraced an option that had seemed so out of reach that morning—I would be one of the two to graduate. I made the decision right then to focus on succeeding instead of on the obstacles. The option for me was crystal clear, and there was no looking back. That spring, I received an award for *Outstanding Intellectual Curiosity* from the College of Communications (ironically from the same professor who had greeted me with those cheery words on my first day). Two years later I sat on stage with two other students from that original class as we received our master's degrees.

Seeking, learning, staying fresh, brainstorming, and mirroring best practices, are all tangible methods for embracing new options. Having a treasure chest of options gives us strength in the face of challenges and allows us to make easier course corrections as we move toward our signature contributions.

Activities to Create Options

1. COFFEE HOUSE CREATIVITY

Identify a challenge/problem/opportunity you are currently experiencing in the office or at home. Sit in a coffee shop with two people who are not connected to that challenge, but are connected to you. For an hour, list nothing but options. When the conversation lags and you are tempted to think—that's it, there are no more options, ask "What else could we do?" After a full sixty minutes of creating NOTHING but options, read your list out loud. Then sleep on it. Review the list of options the next day and divide the list into two sub lists: "Risky" and "Safe". Be willing to test your favorite options from both lists.

2. TINKER TOY POSSIBILITIES

A quick trip to Toys R Us and a canister of Tinker Toys® makes for a great group exercise on creating options. Divide the canister into two or three piles of pieces and divide your team into two or three groups. With a maximum time of ten minutes, instruct your team to create a product prototype using the pieces they have. Step back and watch! When the time expires, invite each group to share its product. Spend 10 to 15 minutes drawing conclusions for a real challenge you face at work, drawn from the lessons learned from the tinker toys.

3. DREAM BINGO

Play this enlightening game with your team at your next department meeting. Invite everyone to bring a list of 12-15 dreams to your meeting. Distribute the Dream BINGO card (template available at www.thepowerofpebbles.com) and invite everyone to complete his or her personal Dream BINGO sheet by:

- Identifying a FREE space on the card
- Entering one of their DREAMS on each of the remaining spaces on their card.

Next, invite someone to share one of his or her DREAMS aloud to the group. Everyone in the room who shares a similar dream to the one shared marks that space off their BINGO card. Continue to play until someone shouts BINGO (a complete horizontal or vertical line of shared dreams).

4. HOW MANY Fs?

Sometimes we are so sure that what we see and observe is the truth. We trust our senses and our brain to interpret incoming messages and we assign meaning we determine must be the RIGHT meaning. Our conscious mind works through the filter of our perceptions and experiences in an attempt to make sense of what is going on around us. Our filters, clouded by our history and experience, make creating options outside of what we know difficult.

This *How Many Fs* exercise is a simple way to illustrate this. (Please visit www.thepowerofpebbles.com to download the template for this exercise.) Set the exercise up by asking the participants to count how many Fs are written in the paragraph and to keep the answer to themselves. Give the group one minute to read and count the Fs and then ask the group for its answers. Chances are you will receive answers ranging from 1-10 Fs. The correct answers are illustrated on the following page.

In most cases, our eyes miss some of the "Fs" that as we read them are pronounced with a different sound—and our sub-conscious mind doesn't register the letter as an "F". This exercise is a great way to open an "option generating" discussion!

Black holes stand at the very edge oF scientiFic theory. Most scientists believe they exist, although many oF oF their theories break down under the extreme conditions within. But ProFessor Cornelius Van Buckstein oF oF the University oF Ushuaia says he knows what you would Find inside, and challenges the traditional idea that gravity would cause you death by "spaghettiFication.

5. STUCK IN AN ELEVATOR

This exercise works especially well with a group of people who are perhaps new to working together or when the group dynamic tends toward the same people participating vs. non-participating. Here is an adapted version of an exercise from comedienne Loretta LaRoche's innovative *Life is Short—Wear your Party Pants* comes the following exercise.

Create the following scenario. You are in an elevator with six other people, when the elevator suddenly stops between floors. The lights flicker and then go out and the air conditioning quits, too. Come up with a list of at least fifty ways you'd fill time while waiting for the elevator to move again. For extra credit, list the first twenty-five things you will do once you get off the elevator. For the gold medal, write the lyrics to a song parody about being stuck in an elevator with six other people.

W = Wonder

When we take the time to notice, really notice, life is amazing and filled with wonder. Beauty exists all around us, from the smile of a child's face to a butterfly meandering in the back yard. Miracles happen every day. And when we take the time to notice, really notice, we make progress each moment toward our goals, objectives, and dreams. According to the Heart Institute, our hearts generate an energy field that is 5,000 times more powerful than the energy our brains produce. Creating our signature contribution involves the connection of our heart.

In leadership, one of our primary roles is to guide the enthusiasm of those we lead to produce results and growth. Stephen Covey aptly describes leadership as: "The act of pouring belief into others until they are compelled to see it themselves." To convey wonder, we must be willing to walk alongside our team, as the following story illustrates.

One of the highlights from a family vacation to Hawaii a few years back was a kayak trip up the Wialua River, combined with a hike through the tropical jungle to an amazing, hidden waterfall. The excursion was definitely hard work—the river current was steady, the hiking trail was sometimes muddy and slippery, and the ever-present tropical warmth could be draining. The reward was worth every effort and filled to the brim with wonder: a pristine waterfall cascading into a clear fern- and flower-lined natural swimming pool, the sights and sounds of the jungle along the way, and the feeling that you've actually touched a genuine, non-tourist part of Hawaii.

Two years earlier, on my first visit to Kauai, I took this same river excursion trip and enjoyed the experience so completely, I determined that the next time I visited Kauai, I'd bring Alex (my then pre-teen, 11-year-old) with me and we would experience the river journey together.

Alex was a little nervous as we pushed away from shore and started up the river. He wasn't sure what lay ahead, either on the river or on the hike. I reassured him that he would be glad we came and described to him what we would see and do. As we traveled up river, Alex relaxed and we found a comfortable pace. He frequently asked me how much farther we had to go, and asked about the various plants and trees along the river and on the hike. Because the scenery and route were familiar to me, I was able to reassure and guide him. For me, the route brought back wonderful memories, and filled me with anticipation because I knew what splendid reward awaited us at the end of the trail. I experienced the wonder and magic of this amazing excursion through new eyes and seeing Alex react with his heart made this journey more dazzling and worthwhile.

On the way back down the river, the wind worked against us, and the paddling in our tandem kayak was much more difficult. Alex needed to take frequent breaks from paddling, but because the landmarks and distance we needed to travel were familiar to me, I was able to persuade him to keep going—that we were "almost there." Later that afternoon, as we nursed our aching shoulders by the pool, we celebrated our accomplishments. For me, the best reward was seeing Alex smile and talk about how cool the river trip was—he felt successful, brave, confident, and filled with the wonder of the experience!

As leaders, we have traveled similar rivers though building our businesses, our best practices, our failures, and our successes. We recognize the landmarks, we've experienced the rewards, we understand the current, we will likely encounter along the way. We work with other leaders who have similar but unique stories from their journeys. We guide new members of our teams as they navigate the river for the first time, and as we experience the river through their eyes, we are reminded of wonderful memories, celebrate successes, and persuade them to keep paddling when the wind blows against them.

Activities to Experience Wonder

1. PHOTO SCAVENGER HUNT

Leave the OFFICE on a sunny Friday afternoon with this fun exercise for experiencing the wonder of your city/town. Google or pick up a travel book and determine a list of eight to ten unique characteristics and places in your city or town. Design a photo scavenger hunt around what you find.

For example, if your city is famous for a particular brand of chocolate, one of the scavenger hunt items could be: "Take a photo of one of your team members opening a bar of YUMMERLICIOUS chocolate." Divide your office into teams, arm each team with a digital camera or cell phone camera, and set the teams loose. The object of the game is to be the team that returns first with all the required photos. It is an amazing exercise to discover some of the hidden treasures of wonder right in our own back yards. Shake it up and have staff meetings in a local park, or in a natural setting: a beautiful garden or in a boat on a pristine lake.

To design your photo scavenger hunt elements, first choose the location (town or city where or near your business office, location of retreat, off site meeting or convention). Consider the following thought starters as you design your scavenger hunt:

- Natural elements or landscaping features
- Architecture in landmarks or historic buildings
- Inventions or unique products developed here
- Parks
- Tourist destinations
- Famous residents
- Movie set locations
- TV Set locations
- Unique music or cultural elements
- Animal life
- Famous foods
- Historically significant locations or events

2. WHOM ARE WE LOOKING FOR?

In the world of business, customers and clients are our reason for existence. Attracting and keeping ideal clients becomes the difference between businesses that succeed and those that do not. First we need to know WHO is best suited for our products and services. Equally important to understand and be able to articulate is HOW we add to the "wonder" they experience in business/life by using what we offer. (A free template for these exercises is available at www.thepowerofpebbles.com.)

WHO IS OUR IDEAL CLIENT? WHOM DO WE SERVE?

Visualize your customers in detail. Make a list of as many of their demographic elements as possible. The more specific and the longer the list, the better.

- Whom do we love working with? What do our customers believe? What do they enjoy? What do they do?
- What keeps our clients up at night? What are their challenges and obstacles? Why would they seek our assistance?
- WHAT DO WE OFFER?
- What solutions do we provide for their challenges and obstacles? How can we help them?
- Do we have a process, method, or program that addresses their needs?
- How do we reach them?
- How is our message remarkable, "rememberable," and repeatable?
- How do we utilize the recommendations and referrals of our ideal clients to others?

3. GLOBAL CELEBRATIONS

Coordinate a virtual round-the-world tour at the office. As a team, determine twelve locations you'd like to visit over the next year and designate a location for each month. Then determine who on the team will be the tour guide for that location and book calendar dates (once per month recommended) for the year as a part of team/staff meetings or as an after-hours networking function. The purpose is to experience some of the wonder of each location (food, music, culture, sites, and other claims to fame). Even better: Invite team members who have visited exotic and exiting locations bring photos and share experiences from their travels! As we reach outside of our routine a little, we begin to notice—really, really notice—how much, how big, and how wonderful our world is. Kind of puts our small, urgent crisis-filled days into proper perspective!

4. HIGH-WIRE TRAPEZE

Open your team meeting by sharing the following quote from wise business guru Stephen Covey: "I look at an organization as a high-wire trapeze act, and today there's no net." Divide the group into teams or with a small group carry on a discussion using the following template as a guide. Remember, as leaders, our job is to guide our teams as they experience the wonder of new discoveries about themselves, about your business, about their wORLD and WORLD. The metaphor of the High-Wire Trapeze as it relates to your business can be like a set of binoculars—bringing far away strategies and objectives into clear and near focus. Here are some possible questions:

- How or why could our organization be described as a "high-wire trapeze act"?
- How or who could we use a "net"?
- What could we do to offer security for those who take "mid-air" risks?
- What leaps of faith can we add to our daily routines in our organization?
- If your life depended on the training/knowledge you've acquired working in our organization, what could you demonstrate?
- What skills would make you feel safer?
- What other "artists" might be willing to join us on the trapeze and what would they bring?
- What might cause you to lose concentration while performing?
- What would it take for our act to receive a standing ovation from the audience?

5. SECRET MENTORS

This mid-long-term exercise is a spin on the concept of secret pals and is particularly useful with teams who have become stale in their thinking—with more senior members (in terms of longevity) feeling they are entitled to be the teachers or have nothing new to learn. In short, this is an exercise for teams who have lost their sense of WONDER. Put all the names of your team—from the janitor to the executives—in a hat. Invite all to pull a name out and ensure no one received his or her own name. Provide each team member with a box of ten to twelve note cards. The concept of a secret mentor is simple: each week, the Secret Mentor writes and sends a note to the drawn team member. The notes can be about anything—the only rule is that the content must be positive. At the end of the ten to twelve weeks, re-assemble the team and ask what members learned from the experience, both as the MENTOR and as the RECIPIENT. Chances are you'll hear a variety of responses, including some who didn't enjoy having to write something every week.

The real intention of this exercise is to pour positive messages into your team members from their colleagues rather than from you. Magic often happens with this dynamic as it is hard to ignore the WONDER of what is all around us as we walk through life, day by day, week by week. By taking time to notice and share, stale thinking and closed minds often give way to a new beginning for positive and productive movement forward.

If team members approach you saying they are stuck or unsure what to write about, remind them of the one rule—the note can be about ANYTHING as long as it's positive. Invite them to think about the previous seven days and find something they did, saw, or felt that was positive. This could be as simple as seeing a beautiful bird singing happily on a tree branch to a finding the perfect gift for a loved one to sharing a favorite quote. With this direction, your stuck team member will likely recall something positive. Invite your team to be on the lookout for the positive in the coming seven days rather than focusing on looking backward.

E = Excellence

When our actions are fueled by our dreams, we naturally elevate the level of effort we apply. The enthusiasm we portray translates into excellence rather than mediocrity. Rather than just doing what's needed … we DO what's possible… what's EXCELLENT.

Take an everyday example of restaurant service. We've all experienced the pampering delights accompanying a restaurant server who creates an excellent dining experience—never letting our water glass drain to less than half full, checking frequently to ensure the meal quality is to our standard and satisfaction, cheerfully recommending favorite dessert items—are common examples of excellent service. And if an element of our meal is not up to par, an excellent server will do whatever it takes to make it right for us—the customers.

Unfortunately, the opposite of excellent service can ruin an otherwise five-star dining experience. Feeling like a burden or a bother, having to wait to be acknowledged, having to ask for the check after being ignored—it's also very easy to spot sub-excellent service.

Being excellent means making your customer's, your team's, or your family's day. Excellence encompasses both giving your BEST effort and attitude as well as exhibiting competence; a productive attitude and effort go hand in hand. Pike Place Market in downtown Seattle exhibits one of the most compelling examples of EXCEL-LENCE in terms of attitude and effort with the world-famous Pike Place Fish Market. Known for throwing fish from the frozen cases across the counter to the guys who weigh and pack the fresh seafood, the workers at Pike Place Fish Market practice their own Fish Philosophy.

Their mantra is based on putting the customer first: making the customer's day, being there, and choosing a positive attitude in everything they do. As one of the fishmongers says: "It's about who you are being while you're doing what you're doing." Even when dealing in with horrid pre-dawn work hours, outdoor working conditions at the market in the damp and dreary Seattle rain, and handling all the aspects of smelly, cold fish, the guys ensure that each customer is treated to excellent service. They acknowledge each customer and genuinely attempt to recommend the best seafood options. They entertain tourists and business people who wander through the market with their engaging fish tosses. Most importantly, they enjoy a prosperous and success-ful business. We like to do business with people who treat us with excellence, and the Pike Place Fish Market is a superb example of this commonly held truth.

We DO our work differently when we are being resentful versus when we are being engaged. Excellence in our work, in our families, in our lives comes from choosing and using a winning, helpful, effective attitude.

Competence is also a vital component of being excellent. When we perform our functions competently, we exhibit skills and knowledge that take us beyond what is adequate. We provide a product or service that is more sought after than that of the competition. While other brands may be less expensive or more readily available in the marketplace, competence sets us apart as EXCELLENT!

(Remember, free templates for the following exercises can be downloaded at www.thepowerofpebbles.com.)

Activities to Experience Excellence

1. 30-MINUTE SUSTAINED SILENT READING (SSR)

Anyone can embark on this activity, and when you commit to being consistent with this exercise, you will become more EXCELLENT in every area of your life—work, family, and personal/spiritual development. Arrange and schedule 30 minutes each day for SSR (sustained silent reading).

I find this exercise easiest to maintain when my 30 minutes happen before I turn on my laptop, dial in to check voice mail, open my day planner, or touch one piece of paper on my desk. Scheduling and sticking to your schedule is the most difficult aspect of this exercise. During the 30 minutes, your assignment is to read.

So much wisdom and excellence has been recorded by so many brilliant people in the silent pages of countless books. Take a book off your bookshelf and start there. If your bookshelf is empty, take a trip to Amazon.com or your local bookstore. Ask your friends, colleagues, and family what book has made the biggest impression on them. If you are still stuck on where to begin, review the Recommended Reading list following this section.

Thirty minutes of SSR every day. Just imagine what excellent ideas you'll gain after just one week. Or a month. Or a year. Wow!

2. WHO ARE YOU BEING?

This enlightening exercise builds on the concept from the Pike Place Fish Market: "It's about who you are being when you are doing what you are doing." Have participants/ teams identify activities they enjoy doing at work, and activities they don't enjoy doing at work. Set a timer for one minute, but before starting the time, ask each team member to choose the activity he or she most enjoys doing at work. Let them know they will have one minute to come up with as many adjectives as they can that best describe who they are being when they are doing that activity.

Before starting the timer, instruct the teams to write as many adjectives as they can think of that describes who they are being when they do that activity. The team with the most adjectives after one minute gets 1 point. Continue playing in one-minute rounds, alternating from the activities they like vs. the activities they don't like. The first team to seven points wins. What they win is up to you (maybe they choose the pizza toppings for group lunch), but before you end the exercise, have a debriefing discussion on lessons learned:

- What impact does "who you are being" have on co-workers, customers, boss, family?
- What percent of the time are we "being" who we want to be at work?
- What could we do as a team to increase this percentage?

3. GO AHEAD, MAKE MY DAY!

Hotel chains asks their customers to fill out cards when they catch one of the employees providing excellent service. Restaurants and retail stores display pictures of the employee of the month. Why not start a similar tradition in your office? Create and decorate a YOU MADE MY DAY box and ask your team to be on the look out for EXCELLENCE in fellow employees.

When employees spot someone going above and beyond, have them submit a card with details on what they observed. Share these at staff meetings and reward the efforts of those who were EXCELLENT with a pre-paid coffee card. A twist on this activity as a leader/manager is to set weekly target for YOU MADE MY DAY cards that you will send out when you spot someone exhibiting a positive or productive attitude and doing more than is "necessary."

4. ALWAYS DO YOUR BEST

In his fabulous book, *The Four Agreements*, author Don Miguel Ruiz develops four personal commitments for living a complete and authentic life (see Recommended Reading). The fourth agreement is simply stated: "Always do your best." Ruiz continues:

> *Doing your best, you are going to live your life intensely. You are*
> *going to be productive, you are going to be good to yourself...to*
> *your community, to everything. When you always do your best,*
> *you take action. Doing your best is taking the action because you*
> *love it, not because you are expecting a reward.*

Consider the quote above as it relates to your personal best—your standard of EXCELLENCE. Journal on the following questions:

- What does doing "your best" mean to you?
- When did "your best" show up this week?
- How were you good to yourself, your community, your everything this week?
- What actions do you take frequently because you love them, not because you are expecting a reward?

5. TORTOISE AND HARE CONFIDENCE

At three locations around the room, post signs with one word each: Tortoise, Hare, and Thoroughbred. Ask members of the group if they remember the famous Aesop's fable about the Tortoise and the Hare. Invite the group to listen carefully to the descriptions of the tortoise, hare, and thoroughbred and read the descriptions aloud.

- Tortoise: Likes to move ahead slowly and steadily. Won't be rushed. Finds strength from pulling in his head. Has a strong and protective shell. Doesn't take unnecessary risks. Prefers life on an even keel without crises. Sets own pace, takes one thing at a time.
- Hare: Moves with quick starts and stops. Produces well under pressure. Finds strength in exploration and challenge. Is fragile, agile, and lucky. Enjoys risks and adventures. Hops from crisis to crisis, is easily distracted. Always has many irons in the fire.

- Thoroughbred: Economy and grace of movement. Varies pace according to situation. Strength comes from top-flight conditioning. Always under control. Thrives on competition and challenge. Has clear goals with mileposts to mark progress. Always has something left for the stretch.

After reading the descriptions, ask group members to stand next to the animal description that best describes them. Have them share within their animal groupings why they chose that particular description of themselves. Other discussion questions may include: Do you always fit in the same category or do you change with different people and/or situations? How would you describe yourself is we were in a room with 25 powerful CEOs? How would this change if we were in a room with 25 college freshman? What animal description would you most like to be? How can we infuse the best characteristics of each of the animal types in our work personalities? How do these animal descriptions relate to being EXCELLENT? How do the animal descriptions relate to the principles of confidence and competence?

R = Reliable Results

Here is where good intentions collide head on with fortitude. These are the stuff annual performance reviews are made of—the tangible, the measurable, the bottom line. Without positive results, companies, relationships, or dreams don't survive In a survival-of-the-fittest world, in order to stand out and help ensure positive results, our primary task is to be reliable. Doing what we say we will do with a clear focus on vital actions contributes to positive and predictable results.

In nearly all the books I've read on success, goal setting and business motivation and coaching, the word action shows up frequently in each author's version of a success formula. Ask yourself what comes first, motivation or action? For anyone who has vowed to become fit or shed unwanted pounds, waiting to be motivated can eat up a lot of unproductive time. Taking action, on the other hand, like making healthier food choices and committing to DOING more physical activity typically results in a feeling of motivation. When we eat better, we feel better. When we feel better, we have more energy. When we have more energy, we are motivated to keep going.

We might not be 100-percent sure of the accuracy of our course in business or in life, but taking action—persistent and consistent action—when combined with a clear intention or desire, will lead us in the direction of our dreams. The action steps we take may seem small, insignificant, or unrelated to our purpose. With the perspective of hindsight, we are sometimes surprised at how small action steps led the way toward big results.

Our dreams, purposes, and intentions also play a vital part in the achievement of reliable results. Intentions are specific, power-filled commitments that we speak or think or believe with fierce conviction. Dr. Wayne Dyer is an expert in exploring the various facets of intention (see Recommended Reading). His definition of intention implies that intention is not something we do, but rather a "force that exists in the Universe as an invisible field of energy." Dyer believes we can each tap into and harness the power of the "dormant forces" that exist in each of us to co-create the lives we deserve to live.

The following is a partial list of additional definitions of "intention" from a conglomeration of sources:

INTENTION:

- A knowingness, a deep clarity with intensity.
- Focus, certainty or commitment
- Your WHAT put into words
- Goals and objectives
- Stepping stones to success

Back to math again. The combination of a clearly defined INTENTION + ACTION = RESULTS. Both elements, intention and action, are necessary to produce reliable and predictable success. It's not enough to have a goal to be fit. We must also be willing to take the actions required to produce results. And those actions must be consistent and repeated or adjusted, over and over, again and again for as long as it takes to reach the desired result. As defined in *The Power of Focus* by Jack Canfield, Mark Victor Hansen and Les Hewitt, "A goal is the ongoing pursuit of a worthy objective until accomplished."

During the DOING of the action steps, it's essential to set up and follow a system of checking in, recording progress made, and making adjustments when necessary. Accountability or a check-in system measures monetary results versus targets, annual performance reviews versus expectations, and heart-to-heart talks with your spouse on the state of the relationship. Accountability check-ins are a chance to review what happened or didn't happen, as well as ensure that we have the knowledge, resources, and motivation to stay true to the goal.

Both success and failure along the way toward the achievement of our reliable results can be expected. We fall off the diet wagon when a dessert looks too tempting, or our goal to read for 30 minutes every day gets side-tracked with meetings and travel schedules. One of the leaders I work with says: "It's OK to quit doing your business for 24 hours." It's OK to say I QUIT as long as you come back to work tomorrow. Remember, the most important key to staying motivated is to take ACTION. Do something every day that engages your intention. Ask yourself each morning:

- What is ONE thing I can do today to move forward in the direction of my dreams?
- What is standing in my way from taking that action right now?

Then, take responsibility for the answers, and take ACTION!

Activities to Create Reliable Results

1. GOOSE-BUMP INTENTIONS

Review the definitions of intention discussed in this section with your team. Invite them to complete the following questions within 48 hours. Matthew Kelly writes about a unique and vital component of effective leadership in his book *The Dream Manager*. Kelly asserts that employees are more loyal and productive when we help them see the connection between the work they do and the achievement of their dreams. He further states that the primary role of every employee is to become the best version of himself or herself. As leaders, we can assist in that process by provide opportunities for our teams to reflect on their intentions and dreams and purposes.

What will give you GOOSEBUMPS when it shows up? Write down what you actually want, not what you think you should want. Be totally honest with yourself.

- What do you want to achieve in the next five years?
- What do you want to achieve in one year?
- What do you want to achieve in the next six months?
- What do you want to achieve in the next month?
- What do you want to achieve in the next week?
- What do you want to achieve today?

2. 90-DAY BENCHMARKS

Staying motivated requires regular accountability check-ins. Achieving reliable results is often easier when we map out the road ahead and pre-identify any road blocks or obstacles. By being clear on what we want to accomplish and the route we plan to take to get there, our journey toward reliable results is a much smoother one. Use the "90 Day Benchmarks" handout as a one-on-one coaching tool with your team members or as an accountability map for your own dreams and intentions.

What's MOST important to you right now? Identify the top three goals you would like to focus on for the next 90 days. From this starting point, indicate both action steps you plan to take and any obstacles you anticipate.

- MOST IMPORTANT GOAL #1:
  - Actions/First Steps:
  - Obstacles:
- REALLY IMPORTANT GOAL #2:
  - Actions/First Steps:
  - Obstacles:
- STILL IMPORTANT GOAL #3:
  - Actions/First Steps:
  - Obstacles:

3. WHERE ARE THE ROADBLOCKS?

Identifying potential road blocks and obstacles ahead of time, as well as proactively deciding how we will jump over, around, and through them, go a long way toward the achievement of our objectives. Surprisingly, many of us struggle with similar road blocks in both personal and business pursuits. With carefully crafted responses: "When this roadblock pops up, I will…," we are better able to turn road blocks into opportunities for strength or success. Sometimes a hindrance can turn into a helping hand. Sometimes what we struggle most with become our greatest strength. The "Roadblocks" exercise is best used as a one-on-one tool. Please download the template at www.thepowerofpebbles.com.

4. HEY, COACH!

Imagine the role of a school basketball coach. Teaching and training on game fundamentals and skills is only a small fraction of his or her job. The more important role comes in pumping up the team, congratulating the players, defending the team against bad calls, making adjustments to the line-up and strategy, and helping call attention to areas of improvement and an opportunity.

As business leaders, a vital part of our role is to coach the members of our team to be winning contributors to the group's overall success. Coaches ask a lot of questions and hold players accountable for their actions. Coaches call regular practices to review "film" and tactics. The same is true for business coaching. Please download the thought-provoking questions for this exercise from www.thepowerofpebbles.com .

5. STEP ON IT!

Are you having difficulty designing a system to keep you accountable to your dreams, while ensuring you are taking consistent and persistent action? Systems are like habits. With repetitive use of an accountability or tracking system, measuring our progress becomes habitual—an automatic action. Systems do not have to be complex to be effective. By using the "Step On It!" method that follows, you are sure to make the most of your thinking and planning time. Implementation and accountability checkpoints will provide you with an accurate picture of what is really happening. You are on your way to producing RELIABLE RESULTS!

S. SCHEDULE —Make a list of each action or sub-project and schedule it. Be as detailed as possible to insure nothing in your objectives is left undone or missing a link. Consider: Who is responsible or best suited to complete this task? Completion target date? Desired outcome?

T. TACKLE — What additional resources are required to tackle the job and get it done? Do you need additional manpower or think-power? Is the amount of time blocked out to work sufficient to get it done? Are you able to work with limited interruptions or distractions?

E. EVALUATE — Review your progress weekly. Are adjustments needed or are you on course? Are you receiving the support and resources you need or is something missing? Are you tracking to complete your objective on time? Can you measure the percent of desired outcome achieved vs. what is still left to complete?

P. PERSEVERE —Keep at it. Daily actions. Ask yourself: "Is what I am doing right now moving me closer to the completion of my objective?" If it is, keep doing it. If not, take a different action.

The P.O.W.E.R. Formula Revisited

Six years ago, a particular set of unrelated actions completely changed my professional direction. This experience contributed to a clearer definition of my purpose, opened unbelievable options, reminded me of wonder, and provided a venue in which to be excellent and produce reliable results.

After the boom and bust of the dot-com business revolution in the Pacific Northwest, I stumbled on a position with a non-profit technology training organization. This small and young organization experienced typical growing pains as we struggled to define ourselves in the marketplace. I fought daily to bring elements of my corporate training background into this new world of non-profit organizations. For a few months, I found my activities to be an exhilarating challenge. As time passed, however, the awareness that I was a round peg trying desperately to fit into a square hole began to wear me down and give me a headache. Without even realizing it, a spiral of negativity began to drag me down and my dreams flickered into dormancy.

One mundane day, an invitation arrived to attend a business awareness conference in Santa Fe, New Mexico. I thumbed through the program specifics and found little that directly related to my role at work. Yet, something about the spirit of the conference appealed to me. A little spark lit somewhere in my heart as I visualized the mystical town of Santa Fe working its magic on me. I was determined to convince my executive director that sending me to the Santa Fe conference would be an excellent use of our center's resources. I prepared a proposal, outlining how I would use the knowledge gained at the conference to the benefit of the organization, highlighting relevant breakout sessions. Finally, I itemized all of the related costs for attendance, making a strong R. O. I. (return on investment) statement and presented my proposal to the executive director. My persuasive persistence and preparation paid off and without any struggle, my request was approved.

Looking back, I remember fuzzy bits and pieces from the sessions I attended at the conference. I recall the chilly, winter-blue Santa Fe sky and the amazing native food. As clear as the pristine water at Fallen Leaf Lake, on the other hand, were the powerful connections I made with the people I met and a Native American stone fetish I found in an out-of-the-way gift shop. These unrelated action steps propelled my professional life into a powerful new direction—one that I wouldn't have been able to predict or anticipate.

The sold-out hotel bursting with the over four hundred conference attendees made the hotel coffee shop very crowded at breakfast on the first day of the conference. The hostess asked if I minded sitting at a table with other parties of one, and in a moment of bravery, I agreed. I sat with a woman who had traveled from St. Louis, Missouri. Pam was a professional trainer and coach who specialized in looking at the various dynamics of time management. Our instant connection quickly blossomed into a friendship. I found Pam fascinating—to me, she lived the life I had dreamed of, doing what she truly loved to do. My dormant dreams began to flicker to life again as Pam and I conversed. I peppered Pam with questions, my fears, and doubts, and pre-determined obstacles over the next three days. She listened and offered the wisdom of her experience. The impression of entrepreneurship and purpose she left on my heart remains a reservoir of strength for me.

On the last full day of the conference, during our afternoon break, Pam and I walked through the streets of downtown Santa Fe in search of souvenirs for our families. The historic plaza blocks held no shortage of shops that carried a wide variety of trinkets and treasures. Pausing in the doorway of one of these shops, I spotted a beautiful display of small stone carvings and stepped inside to take a closer look. That's where I found the badger.

A store clerk was quickly at my side as I marveled at the dozens of small, polished, stone-carved animals. The clerk explained that these stone fetishes were very special—each animal hand carved and created uniquely. As I peered at the small animals, I noticed no two were exactly alike in color, shape, or features. She invited me bend down closer to the table and allow my animal guide to introduce itself. My eyes fell immediately on my badger. I was drawn to his light blue eyes, striking stone stripes running down his back, and a curious bundle of tiny stones and an arrowhead strapped around his waist. His little three-inch body seemed too small for the enormous significance he portrayed in his firm stance.

"That's his prayer bundle," the enthusiastic clerk offered, pointing to the stones and arrowhead. "The artist placed this on his back so Badger's unique message can be heard."

I was hooked. I couldn't help asking: "What is his message?"

She smiled and replied, "Take him home and he will tell you."

I carried the badger home with me in my carry-on luggage, arguing with the TSA officer that the arrowhead on his prayer bundle was not a danger to anyone on my flight. I placed the badger on my desk at home and waited for him to speak his message.

All too soon, I found myself back in my dull and tedious work routine. My daily two-hour commute from Renton, Washington north to Bothell was beginning to turn me into a grump every evening. I found my work meaningless as I reflected on the lessons learned in talking with Pam. I remembered one conversation in particular at lunch at the amazing and historic Café Pasqual in downtown Santa Fe. Slipping into her coaching/training mode, Pam asked me: "When you were a young girl, what did you want to be when you grew up?"

Without hesitation, I replied, "A teacher."

"Hmm. So what changed? Why didn't you become one?"

I thought for a moment, reflecting on the people who advised me as a young girl. "Everyone told me to choose something else—that teachers didn't make any money, weren't respected or appreciated. Everyone said I could do better."

Pam carefully considered my response before asking another, more stinging question: "If being a teacher is really what you want to do, how can you find a way to be one?"

I found myself thinking about Pam's question while staring at my badger. I began to feel resentful—I worked in an unfulfilling job and felt stuck. How could I be a teacher without going back to school for more education? What good did it do to dream of a life beyond corporate America where I could teach and speak and train? Bills to be paid. Obligations to meet.

Within a week of returning from Santa Fe, a curious email popped into my inbox from a recruiter who had seen my resume on Monster.com. His brief message shook the ground around me.

"Hi. I am conducting a search for a regional sales and training manager for an international cosmetics company. From what I see on your resume, your experience aligns with what the employer is seeking. If you are interested in discussing, please contact me."

I remember staring at that message for minutes as fireworks exploded in my head. My first thought was to hit the delete key—cosmetics? Who are we kidding here? Then I glanced over at my badger. Pam's words echoed in my head: "If being a teacher is really what you want to do…" My mother's voice chimed in: "You can do anything…" I heard a oft-repeated quote that had once been my mantra: "Do what you love and the money will follow." Finally, I heard my badger shout: "Go for it!"

I heeded the messages. I took the one small, action step of hitting the Reply button instead of Delete to that email. That action prompted another action and another and a string of others. I looked up the meaning of my Native American totem, my badger, and learned the badger's purpose is to bring boldness, perseverance, and individuality. I discovered that as I opened my heart to exploring new options, my purpose became clearer. I found wonder in an industry I had scarcely acknowledged before. I traded my two-hour daily commute for a 30-second stroll from the kitchen to my home office. My work has meaning and purpose and is never stale or dull. I help women grow and reach toward their dreams. I am a coach. I am a teacher.

WORKS CONSULTED
RECOMMENDED READING

Alpine Sierra Trailblazer, by Jerry and Janine Sprout. Diamond Valley Company, California, 2004.

Developing the Leader Within You, by John C. Maxwell. Injoy Inc., Tennessee, 1993.

Excuse Me, Your Life is Waiting, by Lynn Grabhorn. Hampton Roads Publishing, Virginia, 2000.

Fish!, by Stephen Lundin, Harry Paul and John Christensen. Hyperion, New York, 2000.

Great Session Openers Closers and Energizers, by Marlene Caroselli. McGraw-Hill, New York, 1998.

Hope for the Flowers, by Trina Paulus. Paulist Press, New York, 1972.

Life is Short, Wear Your Party Pants, by Loretta LaRoche. Hay House, Inc., California, 2003.

Managing to Have Fun, by Matt Weinstein. Fireside, New York, 1996.

Re-Imagine!, by Tom Peters. DK Publishers, New York, 2003.

The 8th Habit, by Stephen R. Covey. Free Press, New York, 2004.

The 21 Irrefutable Laws of Leadership, by John C. Maxwell. Injoy Inc., Maxwell Motivation, Inc, Tennessee, 1998.

The Dream Giver, by Bruce Wilkenson. Multnomah Publishers, Inc., Oregon, 2003.

The Dream Manager, by Matthew Kelly. Beacon Publishing, New York, 2007.

The Four Agreements, by Don Miguel Ruiz. Amber-Allen Publishing, Inc., California, 1997.

The Invitation, by Oriah Mountain Dreamer. Harper Collins Publishers, San Francisco, 1999.

The Power of Focus, by Jack Canfield, Mark Victor Hansen and Les Hewitt. Health Communications, Florida, 2000.

The Power of Intention, by Dr. Wayne Dyer. Hay House, Inc., California, 2004.

The Radical Leap, by Steve Farber. Kaplan Publishing, Illinois, 2004.

The Road Less Traveled, by M. Scott Peck. Simon and Schuster, New York, 1978.

Whale Done!, by Ken Blanchard. The Free Press, New York, 2002.

Who Moved My Cheese?, by Spencer Johnson, M.D. G.P. Putnam's Sons, New York, 1998.

About the Author

Pebbles from Fallen Leaf Lake and Other Motivational Moments is Sheryl Hughey's first published book. Sheryl graduated with a Bachelor's and Master's Degree in Communication from Brigham Young University and now lives with her family in Maple Valley, Washington. Sheryl works as National Training Manager for JAFRA Cosmetics, International. She is a motivational speaker and trainer, professional member of the National Speaker's Association, e-Women Network and the Pacific Northwest Writer's Association. To learn more, please visit: www.thepowerofpebbles.com. We would love to hear from you!